Rainbows to

Remind Us

*Great Character
Building Quotations
&
World Proverbs*

Edwina Doyle Willis

Llumina
PRESS

Rainbows to Remind Us

Great Character Building Quotations
&
World Proverbs

© 2017 Edwina Doyle Willis

ISBN: 978-1-62550-332-9

Dedication

For my granddaughters,
Leah Claire Campbell,
Alaina Quinn Campbell,
and Grace Cory Shelby
with hopes that you
will grow up to be
women of great
character and
compassion.

"Try to be a rainbow in someone's cloud."

Maya Angelou

Table of Contents

Preface

"Employ your time in improving yourself by other man's writings so that you shall gain easily what others have labored hard for."

Socrates

Because a country is only as good as its citizens, great countries are created by citizens of great character. Just like the rainbow reminds us of God's promise to us after the Great Flood, the quotes in *Rainbows to Remind Us* help us remember those moral values that enrich families, communities, and countries.

Henry David Thoreau commented during the 19th century that, "The mass of men lead lives of quiet desperation"; sadly, this desperation is even more evident in the 21st century in which young cyber titans have access to infinite knowledge but often lack the wisdom to use it. Random and ridiculous acts of violence plague our peace, and obscene and heinous crimes sabotage our society. Sadly, increasing rates of human trafficking and slavery, bullying, road rage, and other forms of targeted and random violence wreak havoc in our world.

Rainbows to Remind Us: Great Character Building Quotations is a welcome resource in these troubled times. American literary great Henry Wadsworth Longfellow once wrote that, "Into each life some rain must fall." Country music superstar Dolly Parton's spin on that sentiment is, "The way I see it, if you want the rainbow, you gotta put up with the rain." Thankfully, we have rainbows to remind us that after we endure life's rainstorms, we can enjoy sunshine and possibly a radiant kaleidoscopic rainbow.

Instead of having to peruse hundreds of quotations to find a few gems—which is the case with most books of quotations—my strict criterion for inclusion is that each selection is succinct; timely; timeless; encouraging and inspirational; and uttered by a recognizable and respected person. Although these quotations highlighting 67 character traits will sooth, inspire, and encourage the reader, no matter what the age, they are especially useful for the following:

❖ Teachers' prompts for student journals and bell ringers
❖ Ministers' sermons and lessons
❖ Public speakers' speeches and presentations
❖ Youth leaders and camp counselors
❖ Students' essays and speeches
❖ Those who want to make their social media sparkle

Also included is a section of World Proverbs, which is a rich resource of timeless wisdom from all over the world. An alphabetically arranged glossary makes it easy to check the biographical highlights of those quoted.

Another great use for this book is to spark conversation around the dinner table. Former U.S. President Ronald Reagan said, "All great change in America begins at the dinner table." If parents regularly used a quotation to spark conversation, they could encourage communication and thus bond with their family. Focusing on encouraging, inspirational, and wise thoughts can replace negative topics that sometimes make mealtime unpleasant. *Rainbows to Remind Us* is not only the perfect graduation and birthday gift, but it can also encourage friends and family who are suffering because of health challenges, emotional stress, or tragic loss.

Writer E.L. Konigsburg wrote that, "The adventure is over. Everything gets over except the part you carry with you." I hope that you will carry these pithy phrases and tidbits of truth with you throughout your life. Remember that sunflowers hang their heads on the sunny side, so when you desire to live a more magnificent life as a man or woman of virtuous character, turn to the wisdom in *Rainbows to Remind Us*.

Achievement

There is no passion to be found playing small—
in settling for a life that is less than
the one you are capable of living.

Nelson Mandela

The greatest use of life is to spend it
for something that will outlast it.

William James

Happiness lies in the joy of achievement
and the thrill of creative effort.

Franklin D. Roosevelt

I long to accomplish a great and noble task, but
it is my chief duty to accomplish small tasks
as if they were great and noble.

Helen Keller

Genius is seldom recognized for what it is:
a great capacity for hard work.

Henry Ford

When we have accepted the worst, we have nothing more to lose. And that automatically means we have everything to gain.

Dale Carnegie

Success isn't measured by the position we reach in life; it's measured by the obstacles we overcome.

Booker T. Washington

Nothing great was ever achieved without enthusiasm.

Ralph Waldo Emerson

All ambitions are lawful except those that climb upward on the miseries or credulities of mankind.

Joseph Conrad

Keep away from people who try to belittle your ambitions.

Mark Twain

Opportunity is missed by most people because it is dressed in overalls and looks like work.

Thomas Jefferson

Action

The successful person has the habit of doing
the things failures don't like to do.

Thomas Alva Edison

Things may come to those who wait, but
only the things left by those who hustle.

Abraham Lincoln

A life spent making mistakes is not only more honorable
but more useful than a life spent doing nothing.

George Bernard Shaw

God provides the wind, but man must raise the sails.

Saint Augustine

I think one's feelings waste themselves
in words; they ought all to be distilled
into actions which brings results.

Florence Nightingale

The bitterest tears shed over graves are for
words left unsaid and deeds left undone.

Harriet Beecher Stowe

You miss 100% of the shots you don't take.

Wayne Gretzky

In gentle ways, you can shake the world.

Mahatma Gandhi

There are many ways of going forward,
but only one way of standing still.

Franklin Delano Roosevelt

Be always sure you're right, then go ahead.

Davy Crockett

A thousand words leave not the same
deep impression as does a single deed.

Henrik Ibsen

Adversity

Sweet are the uses of adversity, which, like the toad, ugly and venomous, wears yet a precious jewel in his head.

William Shakespeare

When the going gets tough, the tough get going.

Robert Schuller

Little minds are tamed and subdued by misfortune, but great minds rise above it.

Washington Irving

Mishaps are like knives, that either serve us or cut us, as we grasp them by the blade or the handle.

James Russell Lowell

For every ailment under the sun,
There is a remedy, or there is none.
If there be one, try to find it;
If there be none, never mind it.

Dale Carnegie

Many men owe the grandeur of their lives
to their tremendous difficulties.

Charles H. Spurgeon

I would never have amounted to anything were it not
for adversity. I was forced to come up the hard way.

James Cash Penny

Adversity has the same effect on a man
that severe training has on the pugilist—
it reduces him to his fighting weight.

Josh Billings

You can only come to the morning through the shadows.

J.R.R. Tolkien

It is only the women whose eyes have
been washed clear with tears who
get the broad vision that makes
them little sisters to all the world.

Dorothea Dix

Attitude

Attitude is a little thing that makes a big difference.

Winston Churchill

Nothing can stop the man with the right mental attitude from achieving his goal; nothing on earth can help the man with the wrong mental attitude.

Thomas Jefferson

The greatest day in your life and mine is when we take total responsibility for our attitudes. That's the day we truly grow up.

John C. Maxwell

Weakness of attitude becomes weakness of character.

Albert Einstein

People may hear your words, but they feel your attitude.

John C. Maxwell

He can who thinks he can, and he can't who thinks he can't.

Pablo Picasso

We can complain because rose bushes have thorns,
or rejoice because thorn bushes have roses.

Abraham Lincoln

If you don't like something change it; if you can't
change it, change the way you think about it.

Mary Engelbreit

Whatever your situation might be, set your mind to
whatever you want to do and put a good attitude in it, and I
believe that you can succeed. You are not going to get
anywhere just sitting on your butt and moping around.

Bethany Hamilton

I am still determined to be cheerful and happy,
in whatever situation I may be; for I have also
learned from experience that the greater
part of our happiness or misery depends upon our
dispositions, and not upon our circumstances.

Martha Washington

Authenticity

Be yourself; everyone else is already taken.

Oscar Wilde

Do not go where the path may lead; go instead
where there is no path and leave a trail.

Ralph Waldo Emerson

Tell me who admires and loves you,
and I will tell you who you are.

Antoine de Saint Exupéry

Your worth consists in what you
are and not in what you have.

Thomas Alva Edison

You can only lose something that you have;
you cannot lose something that you are.

Eckhart Tolle

It is better to fail in originality
than to succeed in imitation.

Herman Melville

Why fit in when you were born to stand out?

Dr. Seuss

Two roads diverged in a wood,
and I—I took the one less traveled by,
and that has made all the difference.

Robert Frost

None of us will ever accomplish anything excellent
or commanding except when he listens to this
whisper which is heard by him alone.

Ralph Waldo Emerson

Forget what the world thinks of you stepping
out of your place; think your best thoughts,
speak your best words, work your best works,
looking to your own conscience for approval.

Susan B. Anthony

Beauty

Though we travel the world over to find the beautiful,
we must carry it with us or we find it not.

Ralph Waldo Emerson

It is amazing how complete is the
delusion that beauty is goodness.

Leo Tolstoy

A thing of beauty is a joy forever; its loveliness
increases; it will never pass into nothingness.

John Keats

Beauty is not in the face; beauty is a light in the heart.

Kahlil Gibran

Everybody needs beauty as well as bread,
places to play in and pray in, where nature
may heal and give strength to body and soul.

John Muir

People are like stained-glass windows.
They sparkle and shine when the sun is out,
but when the darkness sets in, their true beauty is revealed
only if there is a light from within.

Elisabeth Kübler-Ross

Never lose an opportunity of seeing anything
beautiful, for beauty is God's handwriting.

Ralph Waldo Emerson

The best and most beautiful things in the world cannot be
seen or even touched; they must be felt with the heart.

Helen Keller

Not being beautiful was the true blessing . . . .
not being beautiful forced me to develop my inner
resources. The pretty girl has a handicap to overcome.

Golda Meir

Beauty without grace is the hook without the bait.

Ralph Waldo Emerson

Bullying

A torn jacket is soon mended; but
hard words bruise the heart of a child.

Henry Wadsworth Longfellow

No one heals himself by wounding another.

Saint Ambrose

All cruelty springs from hard-heartedness and weakness.

Marcus Annaeus Seneca

No one can make you feel inferior without your consent.

Eleanor Roosevelt

There are two ways of exerting one's
strength: one is pushing down;
the other is pulling up.

Booker T. Washington

Only the weak are cruel. Gentleness can
only be expected from the strong.

Leo Buscaglia

We either add to the darkness of indifference
or we light a candle to see by.

Madeleine L'Engle

A hurtful act is the transference to others
of the degradation which we bear in ourselves.

Simone Weil

Courage is fire, and bullying is smoke.

Benjamin Disraeli

If you dig a grave for others,
you might fall into it yourself.

Irish Proverb

Nobody can hurt me without my permission.

Mahatma Gandhi

False words are not only evil in themselves,
but they infect the soul with evil.

Socrates

He who commits injustice is ever made
more wretched than he who suffers it.

Plato

He that flings dirt at another dirties himself most.

Thomas Fuller

To make us feel small in the right
way is a function of art; men can
only make us feel small in the wrong way.

E.M. Forster

It has always been a mystery to me
how men can feel themselves honored
by the humiliation of their fellow beings.

Mahatma Gandhi

A man can't ride your back unless it's bent.

Martin Luther King, Jr.

When men speak ill of thee,
live so as nobody may believe them.

Plato

He that undervalues himself will undervalue others,
and he that undervalues others will oppress them.

Samuel Johnson

He who passively accepts evil is as much
involved in it as he who helps to perpetrate it.

Martin Luther King, Jr.

Always stop to think whether your fun may
be the cause of another's unhappiness.

Aesop

You have power over your mind, not outside events.

Marcus Aurelius

Career

The best augury of man's success in his profession
is that he thinks it the finest in the world.

George Eliot

People think at the end of the day that a man is the only
answer [to fulfillment]. Actually a job is better for me.

Diana, Princess of Wales

If you always do what interests you,
then at least one person is pleased.

Katharine Hepburn

Whatever the job you are asked to do at whatever level,
do a good job because your reputation is your resume.

Madeleine Albright

Children are thirsty for a great vision.

Maria Montessori

If a man does not know what port he is
steering for, no wind is favorable to him.

Marcus Annaeus Seneca

The best way to predict the future is to create it.

Abraham Lincoln

I long to accomplish a great and noble task,
but it is my chief duty to accomplish small
tasks as if they were great and noble.

Helen Keller

The high prize of life, the crowning fortune of a man,
is to be born with a bias to some pursuit which
finds him an employment and happiness.

Ralph Waldo Emerson

When men are rightfully occupied, then
their amusement grows out of their work
as the color petals out of a fruitful garden.

John Ruskin

Character

Be more concerned with your character than with your reputation. Your character is what you really are while your reputation is merely what others think you are.

Dale Carnegie

Associate yourself with men of good quality if you esteem your own reputation; for 'tis better to be alone than in bad company.

George Washington

If you will think about what you ought to do for other people, your character will take care of itself.

Woodrow Wilson

Example is not the main thing in influencing others. It is the only thing.

Albert Schweitzer

I look to a day when people will not be judged by the color of their skin, but by the content of their character.

Martin Luther King Jr.

Reputation is what man and women think of us;
character is what God and the angels know of us.

Thomas Paine

What you do when you don't have to, determines
what you will be when you can no longer help it.

Rudyard Kipling

Character is like a tree
and reputation like its shadow.
The shadow is what we think of it;
the tree is the real thing.

Abraham Lincoln

What lies behind us and what lies before us are
tiny matters compared to what lies within us.

Ralph Waldo Emerson

The right way is not always the popular
and easy way. Standing for right when it is
unpopular is a true test of moral character.

Margaret Chase Smith

Happiness is not the end of life; character is.

Henry Ward Beecher

God sends no one away empty except
those who are full of themselves.

Dwight L. Moody

Bodily vigor is good, and vigor of intellect is
even better, but far above both is character.

Theodore Roosevelt

Gross and obscure natures, however decorated,
seem impure shambles; but character gives splendor
to youth and awe to wrinkled skin and gray hairs.

Ralph Waldo Emerson

The ultimate measure of a man is not where he stands
in moments of comfort and convenience, but where
he stands at times of challenge and controversy.

Martin Luther King, Jr.

Character is much easier lost than recovered.

Thomas Paine

Charity

If you can't feed a hundred people, then feed just one.

Mother Teresa

Good works do not make a good man,
but a good man does good works.

Martin Luther

The cistern contains. The fountain overflows.

William Blake

How far that little candle throws his beams.
So shines a good deed in a weary world.

William Shakespeare

The chill of charity is the silence of the heart:
the flame of charity is the clamor of the heart.

Saint Augustine

Charity. To love human beings insofar as they
are nothing. That is to love them as God does.

Simone Weil

The living need charity more than the dead.

George Arnold

Even if it's a small thing, do something for those
who have need of help, something for which
you get no pay but the privilege of doing it.

Albert Schweitzer

Charity begins at home, but should not end there.

Thomas Fuller

Charity, to be fruitful, must cost us.

Mother Teresa

No one has ever become poor by giving.

Anne Frank

25

Compassion

Compassion is the chief law of human existence.

Fyodor Dostoyevsky

Compassion will cure more sins than condemnation.

Henry Ward Beecher

If we could read the secret history of our
enemies, we should find in each man's sorrow
and suffering enough to disarm all hostilities.

Henry Wadsworth Longfellow

If a free society cannot help the many who are
poor, it cannot save the few who are rich.

John F. Kennedy

Yet, taught by time, my heart has learned to glow
for other's good, and melt at other's woe.

Homer

You may call God love, you may call God goodness,
but the best name for God is compassion.

Meister Eckhart

Compassionate people are geniuses in the art of living,
more necessary to the dignity, security, and
joy of humanity than the discoverer of knowledge.

Albert Einstein

We do not need guns and bombs to bring
peace; we need love and compassion.

Mother Teresa

The purpose of life is not to be happy. It is to be
useful, to be honorable, to be compassionate, to make
some difference that you have lived and lived well.

Ralph Waldo Emerson

If you have men who will exclude any of God's creatures
from the shelter of compassion and pity, you will have
men who will deal likewise with their fellow men.

Saint Francis of Assisi

Conduct

Conduct is what we do; character is what we are.

E.M. Bounds

Live with men as if God saw you;
converse with God as if man heard you.

Marcus Annaeus Seneca

Laws control the lesser man. Right
conduct controls the greater one.

Mark Twain

He has honor if he holds himself to an
ideal of conduct though it is inconvenient,
unprofitable, or dangerous to do so.

Walter Lippman

Circumstances are beyond human control,
but our conduct is in our own power.

Benjamin Disraeli

Conviction is worthless unless it is converted into conduct.

Thomas Carlyle

Remember upon the conduct of each
depends the fate of all.

Alexander the Great

The reputation of a thousand years may be
determined by the conduct of a single moment.

Japanese Proverb

I am a radical in thought (and principle)
and a conservative in method (and conduct).

Rutherford B. Hayes

Good manners sometimes means simply
putting up with other people's bad manners.

H. Jackson Brown, Jr.

Friends and good manners will
carry you where money won't go.

Margaret Walker

Confidence

The way to develop confidence is to do the thing you fear and get a record of successful experiences behind you.

William Jennings Bryan

Never bend your head.
Always hold it high.
Look the world straight in the eye.

Helen Keller

You have to have confidence in your ability,
and then be tough enough to follow through.

Rosalynn Carter

One important key to success is self-confidence.
An important key to self-confidence is preparation.

Arthur Ashe

Confidence is contagious; so is lack of confidence.

Vince Lombardi

There can be no friendship without confidence,
and no confidence without integrity.

Samuel Johnson

Whatever we expect with confidence
becomes our own self-fulfilling prophecy.

Brian Tracy

Optimism is the faith that leads to achievement.
Nothing can be done without hope and confidence.

Helen Keller

We must have perseverance and above all
confidence in ourselves. We must believe
that we are gifted for something.

Marie Curie

If you have no self-confidence,
you are twice defeated in the race
of life. With confidence, you have won
even before you have started.

Marcus Gravey

Conscience

A peace above all earthly dignities,
a still and quiet conscience.

William Shakespeare

Labor to keep alive in your breast that little
spark of celestial fire called conscience.

George Washington

It is neither safe nor prudent to
do anything against the conscience.

Martin Luther

There is only one way to achieve happiness
on this terrestrial ball, and that is to
have a clear conscience or none at all.

Ogden Nash

A good conscience is a continual Christmas.

Benjamin Franklin

The human voice can never reach the distance that is covered by the still small voice of conscience.

Mahatma Gandhi

Shame arises from the fear of man,
conscience from the fear of God.

Samuel Johnson

A good conscience is to the soul what health is to the body; it preserves constant ease and serenity within us.

Joseph Addison

There is a higher court than courts of justice and that is the court of conscience. It supersedes all other courts.

Mahatma Gandhi

There is no pillow so soft as a clear conscience.

French Proverb

The person who loses their conscience
has nothing left worth keeping.

Izaak Walton

Cooperation

All for one, one for all, that is our motto.

Alexandre Dumas

We must live together as brothers
or perish together as fools.

Martin Luther King, Jr.

Liberty *and* Union, now and forever, one and inseparable.

Daniel Webster

No man is an island, entire of itself;
every man is a piece of the continent.

John Donne

One hand washes the other.

Seneca

If you want to make peace with your enemy,
you have to work with your enemy.
Then he becomes your partner.

Nelson Mandela

Competition has been shown to be useful
up to a certain point and no further, but
cooperation, which is the thing we must strive
for today, begins where competition leaves off.

Franklin D. Roosevelt

Though force can protect in emergency, only
justice, fairness, consideration and cooperation
can finally lead men to the dawn of eternal peace.

Dwight D. Eisenhower

Nothing truly valuable can be achieved except by
the unselfish cooperation of many individuals.

Albert Einstein

Alone we can do so little; together we can do so much.

Helen Keller

Courage

Courage is fear holding on a minute longer.

George S. Patton

Courage is going from failure to failure
without losing enthusiasm.

Winston Churchill

He is courageous who endures and fears
the right thing, for the right motive, in
the right way and at the right times.

Aristotle

Courage is not having the strength to go on; it
is going on when you don't have the strength.

Theodore Roosevelt

You gain strength, courage, and confidence
by every experience in which you stop
to look fear directly in the face.

Eleanor Roosevelt

One man with courage makes a majority.

Andrew Jackson

Courage is what it takes to stand up and speak;
courage is also what it takes to sit down and listen.

Winston Churchill

It takes a great deal of courage to stand up to your
enemies, but even more to stand up to your friends.

J.K. Rowling

Courage doesn't mean you don't get afraid.
Courage means you don't let fear stop you.

Bethany Hamilton

He who has courage and faith will never perish in misery.

Anne Frank

When a brave man takes a stand, the
spines of others are often stiffened.

Billy Graham

Courtesy

Courtesy is as much a mark of a gentleman as courage.

Theodore Roosevelt

Life is not so short but that there
is always time for courtesy.

Ralph Waldo Emerson

Civility costs nothing but buys everything.

Lady Mary Worley Montagu

A true gentleman is one who is never unintentionally rude.

Oscar Wilde

Courtesies of a small and trivial character
are the ones which strike deepest in the
grateful and appreciative heart.

Henry Clay

When restrain and courtesy are added to
strength, the latter becomes irresistible.

Mahatma Gandhi

Intelligence and courtesy not always are combined;
often in a wooden house a golden room is found.

Henry Wadsworth Longfellow

When music and courtesy are better understood
and appreciated, there will be no war.

Confucius

If a man be gracious and courteous to strangers,
it shows he is a citizen of the world.

Francis Bacon

A man's manners are a mirror
in which he shows his portrait.

Johann Wolfgang von Goethe

No one is too big to be courteous, but some are too little.

Ralph Waldo Emerson

Determination

Do what you can, with what you have, where you are.

Theodore Roosevelt

The greater danger for most of us lies not in setting our aim too high and falling short; but in setting our aim too low, and achieving our mark.

Michelangelo

Big shots are only little shots who kept on shooting.

Dale Carnegie

The difference between an unsuccessful man and others is not a lack of strength, not a lack of knowledge, but rather a lack of will.

Vince Lombardi

Do just once what others say you can't do, and you will never pay attention to their limitations again.

Captain James Cook

40

Never let the fear of striking out get in your way.

Babe Ruth

Life is like riding a bicycle. To keep
your balance, you must keep moving.

Albert Einstein

Anyone can do something when they want to do it. Really
successful people do things when they don't want to do it.

Dr. Phil McGraw

I hated every minute of training but I said, "Don't quit.
Suffer now and live the rest of your life as a champion."

Muhammad Ali

Continuous effort—not strength or intelligence
is the key to unlocking our potential.

Winston Churchill

Strength does not come from physical capacity.
It comes from an indomitable will.

Mahatma Gandhi

41

Discipline

I fear not the man who has practiced 10,000 kicks once, but I fear the man who has practiced one kick 10,000 times.

Bruce Lee

With self-discipline most anything is possible.

Theodore Roosevelt

Discipline is the bridge between goals and accomplishment.

Jim Rohn

Rule your mind or it will rule you.

Horace

By failing to prepare, you are preparing to fail.

Benjamin Franklin

What lies in our power to do lies in our power not to do.

Aristotle

Self-discipline is that which, next to virtue, truly
and essentially raises one man above another.

Joseph Addison

When in doubt, restrain yourself.

Arabian Proverb

There is only one corner of the universe you can be
certain of improving, and that's your own self.

Aldous Huxley

In reading the lives of great men,
I found that the first victory
they won was over themselves;
self-discipline with all of them came first.

Harry S. Truman

The happiness of a man in this
life does not consist in the absence
but in the mastery of his passions.

Alfred Lord Tennyson

Education

A woman without an education is
like a bicycle without a chain.

Malala Yousafzai

It is the mark of an educated mind to be able
to entertain a thought without accepting it.

Aristotle

Education is not the filling of a pail,
but the lighting of a fire.

William Butler Yeats

No man should bring children into the world
who is unwilling to persevere to the end
in their nature and education.

Plato

Education is an ornament in prosperity
and a refuge in adversity.

Aristotle

Education is the ability to listen to almost anything
without losing your temper or self-confidence.

Robert Frost

One child, one teacher, one book
and one pen can change the world.

Malala Yousafzai

He who opens a school door, closes a prison.

Victor Hugo

The educated differ from the uneducated
as much as the living from the dead.

Aristotle

Intelligence plus character—
that is the goal of true education.

Martin Luther King, Jr.

Those who educate children well are more to be
honored than they who produce them; for these
only gave them life, those the art of living well.

Aristotle

A child without education is like a bird without wings.

Tibetan Proverb

Education is teaching our children
to desire the right things.

Plato

So let us wage a glorious struggle against illiteracy,
poverty, and terrorism; let us pick up our books and
our pens. They are the most powerful weapons.

Malala Yousafzai

But if you ask what is the good of education in
general, the answer is easy: that education makes
good men, and that good men act nobly.

Plato

The highest education is that which does
not merely give us information but makes our
life in harmony with all existence.

Rabindranath Tagore

Children must be taught how to think, not what to think.

Margaret Mead

The fate of empires depends on the education of youth.

Aristotle

So please, oh PLEASE, we beg, we pray,
go throw your TV set away,
and in its place you can install
a lovely bookshelf on the wall.

Ronald Dahl

Prejudices . . . are the most difficult to
eradicate from the heart whose soil has never
been loosened or fertilized by education.

Charlotte Bronte

Every time you stop a school, you will have to build a jail.
What you gain at one end you lose at the other. Its' like
feeding a dog on his own tail. It won't fatten the dog.

Mark Twain

Encouragement

Correction does much, but encouragement does more.

Johann Wolfgang von Goethe

At times, our own light goes out and is
rekindled by a spark from another person.

Albert Schweitzer

There are two ways of spreading light; to
be the candle or the mirror that reflects it.

Edith Wharton

Keep away from people who try to belittle your ambitions.
Small people always do that, but the really great
make you feel that you, too, can become great.

Mark Twain

If you want to lift yourself up, lift up someone else.

Booker T. Washington

The greatest good you can do for another is not just share your riches but reveal to him his own.

Benjamin Disraeli

To keep a lamp burning we have to put oil in it.

Mother Teresa

Everyone has an invisible sign hanging from their neck saying, "Make me feel important. Never forget this message when working with people.

Mary Kay Ash

No one is useless in the world who lightens the burden of it for anyone else.

Charles Dickens

It is the true duty of every man to promote the happiness of his fellow creature to the utmost of his power.

William Wilberforce

Faith

Faith is taking the first step even when
you don't see the whole staircase.

Martin Luther King Jr.

To one who has faith no explanation is necessary.
To one without faith, no explanation is possible.

Saint Thomas Aquinas

Every tomorrow has a handle. We can take hold of it
with the handle of anxiety or the handle of faith.

Henry Ward Beecher

Without faith man becomes sterile, hopeless
and afraid to the very core of his being.

Erich Fromm

Reason is our soul's left hand, faith the right.

John Donne

Understanding is the reward of faith.
Therefore seek not to understand
that we may believe, but believe
that you may understand.

Saint Augustine

Faith sees the invisible, believes the
unbelievable, and receives the impossible.

Corrie ten Boom

All I have seen teaches me to trust
the Creator for all I have not seen.

Ralph Waldo Emerson

Faith is the art of holding on
to things your reason has once
accepted, in spite of
your changing moods.

C.S. Lewis

A faith is a necessity to a man.
Woe to him who believes in nothing.

Victor Hugo

Forgiveness

Forgiveness is the fragrance the violet
sheds on the heel that has crushed it.

Mark Twain

Without forgiveness, there's no future.

Desmond Tutu

A wise man will make haste to forgive,
because he knows the true value of time and
will not suffer it to pass away in unnecessary pain.

Samuel Johnson

Forgiveness is not an occasional act;
it is a permanent attitude.

Martin Luther King, Jr.

To err is human, to forgive, divine.

Alexander Pope

An eye for an eye only ends up
making the whole world blind.

Mahatma Gandhi

"I can forgive, but I cannot forget" is only another
way of saying, "I will not forgive." Forgiveness ought
to be like a cancelled note—torn in two and burned
up so that it never can be shown against one.

Henry Ward Beecher

We must develop and maintain the capacity
to forgive. He who is devoid of the power
to forgive is devoid of the power to love.

Martin Luther King, Jr.

The weak can never forgive. Forgiveness
is the attribute of the strong.

Mahatma Gandhi

In one bold stroke forgiveness obliterates the past
and permits us to enter the land of new beginnings.

Billy Graham

Friendship

A friend is one who walks in when
the rest of the world walks out.

Walter Winchell

My best friend is the one who brings out the best in me.

Henry Ford

Grief can take care of itself, but to get the full value
of joy you must have somebody to divide it with.

Mark Twain

One loyal friend is worth 10,000 relatives.

Euripides

The key is to keep company only with people who
uplift you, whose presence calls forth your very best.

Epictetus

There is no friend like an old friend who
has shared our morning days, no greeting
like his welcome, no homage like his praise.

Oliver Wendell Holmes, Sr.

A friend is a person with whom I may be
sincere. Before him, I may think aloud.

Ralph Waldo Emerson

Lots of people want to ride with you in the limo,
but what you want is someone who will take
the bus with you when the limo breaks down.

Oprah Winfrey

Friends . . . they cherish one another's hopes.
They are kind to one another's dreams.

Henry David Thoreau

Friendship is born at that moment
when one person says to another,
"What! You too? I thought I was the only one."

C.S. Lewis

Generosity

Give what you have. To some it may
be better than you dare think.

Henry Wadsworth Longfellow

Lay hold of something that will help you,
and then use it to help somebody else.

Booker T. Washington

It's not how much we give but
how much love we put into giving.

Mother Teresa

No one is useless in this world who
lightens the burden of it for anyone else.

Charles Dickens

You can give without loving, but
you cannot love without giving.

Amy Carmichael

56

If you have two shirts in your closet, one belongs
to you and the other to the man with no shirt.

Saint Ambrose

Gentleness, self-sacrifice and generosity are
the exclusive possession of no one religion.

Mahatma Gandhi

That's what I consider true generosity. You give your
all and yet you always feel as if it costs you nothing.

Simone de Beauvoir

I do not believe one can settle how much
we ought to give. I am afraid the only safe
rule is to give more than we can spare.

C. S. Lewis

You make a living by what you earn,
you make a life by what you give.

Winston Churchill

Goals

Great minds have purposes, others have wishes.

Washington Irving

An aim in life is the only fortune worth finding.

Jacqueline Kennedy Onassis

The true worth of a man is to be
measured by the objects he pursues.

Marcus Aurelius

Our plans miscarry because they have no aim.
When a man does not know what harbor he
is making for, no wind is the right wind.

Lucius Marcus Seneca

There are three ingredients in the good
life: learning, earning, and yearning.

Christopher Morley

He turns not back who is bound to a star.

Leonardo da Vinci

Man's reach should exceed his grasp,
or what's a heaven for?

Robert Browning

The person without a purpose
is like a ship without a rudder.

Thomas Carlyle

Living without an aim is like sailing without a compass.

Alexander Dumas

A goal is not always meant to be reached;
it often serves simply as something to aim at.

Bruce Lee

A good goal is like a strenuous exercise;
it makes you stretch.

Mary Kay Ash

Goodness

Do your little bit of good where you are. Little bits of good that are put together overwhelm the world.

Desmond Tutu

Not only must we be good, but
we must be good for something.

Henry David Thoreau

Each person's task in life is to become
an increasingly better person.

Leo Tolstoy

Confidence in the goodness of another
is good proof of one's own goodness.

Michel de Montaigne

In spite of everything, I still believe
people are really good at heart.

Anne Frank

Find the good. It's all around you. Find it,
showcase it and you'll start believing in it.

Jesse Owens

Non-cooperation with evil is as much
a duty as is cooperation with good.

Mahatma Gandhi

How far that little candle throws its beams!
So shines a good deed in a naughty world.

William Shakespeare

There is never an instant's truce
between virtue and vice. Goodness
is the only investment that never fails.

Henry David Thoreau

Of all virtues and dignities of the
mind, goodness is the greatest.

Francis Bacon

Gossip

Great minds discuss ideas. Average minds
discuss events. Small minds discuss people.

Eleanor Roosevelt

Four horses cannot overtake the tongue.

Chinese Proverb

Gossip is a sort of smoke that comes from the dirty
tobacco pipes of those who diffuse it; it provides
nothing but the bad taste of the smoker.

George Eliot

Gossip is like coal: if it does not char,
at least it will blacken.

Slovakian Proverb

If you reveal your secrets to the wind, you should
not blame the wind for revealing them to the trees.

Kahlil Gibran

If your mouth turns into a knife, it will cut off your lips.

Zimbabwean Proverb

Be less curious about people and more curious about ideas.

Marie Curie

Violence of the tongue is very real—
sharper than any knife.

Mother Teresa

And all who told it added something new,
and all who heard it made enlargements too.

Alexander Pope

It is kind of silly to think that tearing
someone else down builds you up.

Sean Covey

If I maintain my silence about my secret, it is my prisoner.
If I let it slip from my tongue, I am its prisoner.

Arthur Schopenhauer

Gratitude

Gratitude is the fairest blossom
which springs from the soul.

Henry Ward Beecher

If the only prayer you ever say in your
entire life is thank you, it will be enough.

Meister Eckhart

He is a wise man who does not grieve for the things
which he has not, but rejoices for those which he has.

Epictetus

When I first open my eyes upon the morning meadows and
look out upon the beautiful world, I thank God I am alive.

Ralph Waldo Emerson

The worship most acceptable to God
comes from a thankful and cheerful heart.

Plutarch

64

Let gratitude be the pillow upon which
you kneel to say your nightly prayer.
And let faith be the bridge you build
to overcome evil and welcome good.

Maya Angelou

Most human beings have an almost infinite
capacity for taking things for granted.

Aldous Huxley

Appreciation is a wonderful thing; it makes what
is excellent in others belong to us as well.

Voltaire

The thankful receiver bears a plentiful harvest. Where
mercy, love, and pity dwell, there God is dwelling too.

William Blake

I would maintain that thanks are the highest
form of thought, and that gratitude is
happiness doubled by wonder.

G.K. Chesterton

ᏝHappiness

I have learned to seek my happiness by limiting my
desires, rather than in attempting to satisfy them.

John Stuart Mill

The foolish man seeks happiness in the
distance, the wise grows it under his feet.

James Oppenheim

Many persons have a wrong idea of what constitutes true
happiness. It is not attained through self-gratification
but through fidelity to a worthy purpose.

Helen Keller

If you want to be happy, set a goal that commands your
thoughts, liberates your energy and inspires your hopes.

Andrew Carnegie

Happiness is when what you think, what
you say, and what you do are in harmony.

Mahatma Gandhi

The happiness of life is made up of minute fractions—
the little soon forgotten charities of a kiss or smile,
a kind look, a heartfelt compliment.

Samuel Taylor Coleridge

Happiness is a perfume you cannot pour on others
without getting a few drops on yourself.

George Bernard Shaw

Happiness is the gradual realization
of a worthy ideal or goal.

Florence Nightingale

The greatest part of our happiness depends
on our dispositions, not our circumstances.

Martha Washington

If you ever find happiness by hunting for it,
you will find it, as the old woman did her lost
spectacles, safe on her own nose all the time.

Josh Billings

Health

A wise man should consider that health is the greatest of human blessings, and learn by his own thought to derive benefit from his illness.

Hippocrates

The greatest wealth is health.

Virgil

Eat to live, not live to eat.

Benjamin Franklin

Walking is man's best medicine.

Hippocrates

Our growing softness, our increasing lack of physical fitness, is a menace to our security.

John F. Kennedy

It is health that is real wealth
and not pieces of gold and silver.

Mahatma Gandhi

Greedy eaters dig their graves with their teeth.

French Proverb

As I see it, every day you do one of two things:
build health or produce disease in your life.

Adelle Davis

The sum of the whole is this: walk and be
happy; the best way to lengthen out our
days is to walk steadily and with a purpose.

Charles Dickens

The common ingredients of health and long life are:
great temperance, open air, easy labor, little care.

Philip Sidney

Honesty

The honest man takes pains, and then enjoys pleasures, the knave takes pleasure and then enjoys pain.

Benjamin Franklin

Honesty is the first chapter in the book of wisdom.

Thomas Jefferson

I hope I shall always possess firmness and virtue enough to maintain what I consider the most enviable of all titles, the character of an honest man.

George Washington

No legacy is so rich as honesty.

William Shakespeare

An honest man's the noblest work of God.

Alexander Pope

If I ever said in grief or pride,
I tired of honest things, I lied.

Edna Saint Vincent Millay

Truth is proper and beautiful at all times and in all places.

Frederick Douglass

Honesty is the cornerstone of all success, without which
confidence and ability to perform shall cease to exist.

Mary Kay Ash

Rather fail with honor than succeed by fraud.

Sophocles

Oh, what a tangled web we weave,
when first we practice to deceive!

Sir Walter Scott

To make your children capable of honesty
is the beginning of education.

John Ruskin

Honor

Where there is a brave man, in the thickest
of the fight, there is the post of honor.

Henry David Thoreau

Fame is something which must be won;
honor is something which must not be lost.

Arthur Schopenhauer

I could not love thee, dear so much,
loved I not honor more.

Richard Lovelace

Honor lies in honest toil.

Grover Cleveland

It is better to deserve honors and not have
them than to have them and not deserve them.

Mark Twain

Rather fail with honor than succeed by fraud.

Sophocles

If you honor and serve the people who work
for you, they will honor and serve you.

Mary Kay Ash

A man has honor if he holds himself to an
ideal of conduct, though it is inconvenient,
unprofitable, or dangerous to do so.

Walter Lippman

Dignity does not consist in possessing
honors but in deserving them.

Aristotle

No person was ever honored
for what he received. Honor
has been the reward for what he gave.

Calvin Coolidge

Hope

Hope springs eternal in the human breast.
Man never is, but always to be blest.

Alexander Pope

The natural flights of the human mind are not from
pleasure to pleasure, but from hope to hope.

Samuel Johnson

If you do not hope, you will not find
what is beyond your hopes.

Saint Clement of Alexandria

We must accept finite disappointment,
but we must never lose infinite hope.

Martin Luther King, Jr.

Within us we have a hope which always walks
in front of our present narrow experience;
it is the undying faith in the infinite in us.

Rabindranath Tagore

Hope swells my sail.

James Montgomery

Hope is the thing with feathers,
that perches in the soul,
And sings the tune without the words,
and never stops at all.

Emily Dickinson

When hope is taken away from the people,
moral degeneration follows swiftly after.

Pearl S. Buck

If winter comes, can spring be far behind?

Percy Bysshe Shelley

Hope is the word which God has
written on the brow of every man.

Victor Hugo

Humility

Be not proud of race, face, place, or grace.

Samuel Rutherford

I believe the first test of a
truly great man is his humility.

John Ruskin

Too many people overvalue what they
are not and undervalue what they are.

Malcolm S. Forbes

It is not titles that honor men, but men that honor titles.

Niccolò Machiavelli

A true genius admits that he knows nothing.

Albert Einstein

Deeds will not be less valiant because they are unpraised.

J.R.R. Tolkein

After crosses and losses men grow humbler and wiser.

Benjamin Franklin

Sense shines with a double luster when it is set in humility.
An able and yet humble man is a jewel worth a kingdom.

William Penn

A great man is always willing to be little.

Ralph Waldo Emerson

True humility is not thinking less of yourself;
it is thinking of yourself less.

C.S. Lewis

It is always the secure who are humble.

G.K. Chesterton

Humor

Humor is not a trick, not jokes. Humor is a presence
in the world—like grace—and shines on everybody.

Garrison Keillor

A good laugh overcomes more difficulties and
dissipates more dark clouds than any other one thing.

Laura Ingalls Wilder

Humor is emotional chaos remembered in tranquility.

James Thurber

Mirth is God's medicine.

Henry Ward Beecher

The saving grace of America lies in the fact that
the overwhelming majority are possessed of two great
qualities—a sense of humor and a sense of proportion.

Franklin Delano Roosevelt

Humor is the great thing, the saving thing. The minute it crops up, all our irritation and resentments slip away, and a sunny spirit takes their place.

Mark Twain

Good humor is one of the preservatives of our peace and tranquility.

Thomas Jefferson

A person without a sense of humor is like a wagon without springs. It's jolted by every pebble on the road.

Henry Ward Beecher

A well-developed sense of humor is the pole that adds balance to your steps as you walk the tightrope of life.

William Arthur Ward

If I were given the opportunity to present a gift to the next generation, it would be the ability for each individual to learn to laugh at himself.

Charles Schulz

Integrity

The time is always right to do what is right.

Martin Luther King, Jr.

Dare to begin! He who postpones living rightly
is like the rooster who waits for the river
to run out before he crosses.

Horace

A little integrity is better than any career.

Ralph Waldo Emerson

Integrity simply means a willingness
not to violate one's identity.

Erich Fromm

This above all: to thine own self be true,
and it must follow, as the night the day,
thou canst not then be false to any man.

William Shakespeare

Integrity without knowledge is weak and useless, and knowledge without integrity is dangerous and dreadful.

Samuel Johnson

There is no right way to do a wrong thing.

Harold S. Kushner

Be sure you put your feet in the
right place; then stand firm.

Abraham Lincoln

You can preach a better sermon with
your life than with your lips.

Oliver Goldsmith

In matters of style, swim with the current;
in matters of principle, stand like a rock.

Thomas Jefferson

Real integrity is doing the right thing, knowing that
nobody's going to know whether you did it or not.

Oprah Winfrey

Justice

If you are neutral in situations of injustice,
you have chosen the side of the oppressor.

Desmond Tutu

There is no virtue so truly great and godlike as justice.

Joseph Addison

If we expect others to rely on our fairness and justice,
we must show that we rely on their fairness and justice.

Calvin Coolidge

Every step toward the goal of justice
requires sacrifice, suffering, and strength.

Martin Luther King, Jr.

All virtue is summed up in dealing justly.

Aristotle

Justice is justly represented blind, because she sees no difference in the parties concerned. She has but one scale and weight, for rich and poor, great and small.

William Penn

Justice is a machine that, when someone has once given it the starting push, rolls on of itself.

John Galsworthy

These are the laws of justice: That the strong may not oppress the weak, to give justice to the orphan and the widow.

Hammurabi

Justice consists not in being neutral between right and wrong, but in finding out the right and upholding it, wherever found, against the wrong.

Theodore Roosevelt

The moral arc of the universe is long, but it bends toward justice.

Martin Luther King, Jr.

Kindness

You cannot do a kindness too soon, for
you never know how soon it will be too late.

Ralph Waldo Emerson

A kind and compassionate act is often its own reward.

William Bennett

No one is useless in this world who
lightens the burden of others.

Charles Dickens

Carry out a random act of kindness, with no
expectation of reward, safe in the knowledge
that one day someone might do the same for you.

Diana, Princess of Wales

Human kindness has never weakened the stamina
or softened the fiber of a free people.
A nation does not have to be cruel to be tough.

Franklin D. Roosevelt

Kindness is the language, which the
deaf can hear and the blind can see.

Mark Twain

I expect to pass through life but once.
If, therefore, there be any kindness I can show,
or any good thing I can do for any fellow being,
let me do it now . . . as I shall not pass this way again.

William Penn

If you treat people right, they will
treat you right 99% of the time.

Franklin Delano Roosevelt

No act of kindness, no matter how small, is ever wasted.

Aesop

Constant kindness can accomplish much. As the sun
makes ice melt, kindness causes misunderstanding,
mistrust and hostility to evaporate.

Albert Schweitzer

Knowledge

Knowledge itself is power.

Francis Bacon

It is the province of knowledge to speak,
and it is the privilege of wisdom to listen.

Oliver Wendell Holmes, Sr.

Nothing in all the world is more dangerous than
sincere ignorance and conscientious stupidity.

Martin Luther King, Jr.

Nobody cares how much you know,
until they know how much you care.

Theodore Roosevelt

Knowing is not enough; we must apply.
Willing is not enough; we must do.

Johann Wolfgang von Goethe

Ignorance, the root and stem of all evil.

Plato

True knowledge comes only through suffering.

Elizabeth Barrett Browning

The greater our knowledge increases
the more our ignorance unfolds.

John F. Kennedy

You don't have to burn books to destroy a
culture. Just get people to stop reading them.

Mahatma Gandhi

Education is that which discloses to the wise and
disguises from the foolish their lack of understanding.

Ambrose Bierce

An investment in knowledge pays the best interest.

Benjamin Franklin

Leadership

A great leader's courage to fulfill his
vision comes from passion, not position.

John C. Maxwell

Leadership is the art of getting someone else to do
something you want done because he wants to do it.

Dwight Eisenhower

If your actions inspire others to dream more, learn
more, do more, and become more, you are a leader.

John Quincy Adams

He who has never learned to obey
cannot be a good commander.

Aristotle

A true leader has the confidence to stand alone,
the courage to make tough decisions, and the
compassion to listen to the needs of others.

Douglas MacArthur

The art of leadership is saying no, not
saying yes. It is very easy to say yes.

Tony Blair

A good leader is a person who takes a little
more than his share of the blame and
a little less than his share of the credit.

John C. Maxwell

Management is efficiency in climbing the ladder
of success; leadership determines whether the
ladder is leaning against the right wall.

Stephen Covey

I forgot to shake hands and be friendly.
It was an important lesson about leadership.

Lee Iacocca

The greatest leader is not necessarily the one
who does the greatest things. He is the one that
gets the people to do the greatest things.

Ronald Reagan

Love

If you judge people, you have no time to love them.

Mother Teresa

Love does not dominate; it cultivates.

Johann Wolfgang Goethe

Love does not consist in gazing at each other,
but in looking together in the same direction.

Antoine de Saint-Exupéry

Love must be as much a light, as it is a flame.

Henry David Thoreau

To show great love for God and our neighbor we need not
do great things. It is how much love we put in the doing
that makes our offering something beautiful for God.

Mother Teresa

He prayeth best who loveth best
all things both great and small.

Samuel Taylor Coleridge

Love is the only force capable of
transforming an enemy into a friend.

Martin Luther King, Jr.

'Tis better to have loved and lost
Than never to have loved at all.

Lord Alfred Tennyson

Love does not claim possession,
but gives freedom.

Rabindranath Tagore

Darkness cannot drive out darkness;
only light can do that. Hate cannot
drive out hate; only love can do that.

Martin Luther King, Jr.

Loyalty

Lack of loyalty is one of the major
causes of failure in every walk of life.

Napoleon Hill

Faithless is he that says farewell when the road darkens.

J.R.R. Tolkien

In the face I see the map of honour, truth and loyalty.

William Shakespeare

One loyal friend is worth ten thousand relatives.

Euripides

The loyalty of dogs prove there is human potential.

Charles Schultz

What's most important in a friendship?
Tolerance and loyalty.

J.K. Rowling

I'll take fifty percent efficiency
to get one hundred percent loyalty.

Samuel Goldwyn

The scholar does not consider gold and jade to be
precious treasures, but loyalty and good faith.

Confucius

Loyalty is what we seek in friendship.

Marcus Tullius Cicero

In the end, we will remember not the words of
our enemies, but the silence of our friends.

Martin Luther King, Jr.

Loyalty is more valuable than diamonds.

Philippine Proverb

You can easily judge the character of a man by
how he treats those who can do nothing for him.

Johann Wolfgang von Goethe

Manners

There is always a better way of doing everything, if it be to boil an egg. Manners are the happy way of doing things.

Ralph Waldo Emerson

Civility costs nothing and buys everything.

Lady Mary Wortley Montagu

Frame your manners to the time.

William Shakespeare

Respect for ourselves guides our morals; respect for others guides our manners.

Laurence Sterne

The real test of good manners is to be able to put up with bad manners pleasantly.

Kahlil Gibran

God gave you a gift of 84,600 seconds today.
Have you used one of them to say thank you?

William Arthur Ward

Manners are a sensitive awareness of the
feelings of others. If you have awareness, you
have good manners, no matter what fork you use.

Emily Post

A man's manners are a mirror
in which he shows his portrait.

Johann Wolfgang von Goethe

Manners are not idle, but the fruit
of loyal nature and of noble mind.

Alfred Lord Tennyson

Good manners is the art of making those people
easy with whom we converse. Whoever makes the
fewest people uneasy is the best bred in the room.

Jonathan Swift

Modesty

Modesty is the conscience of the body.

Honoré de Balzac

A just and reasonable modesty does not only
recommend eloquence, but sets off every great
talent which a man can be possessed of.

Joseph Addison

Modesty forbids what the law does not.

Marcus Annaeus Seneca

Thy modesty's a candle to thy merit.

Henry Fielding

Modesty is not only an ornament,
but also a guard to virtue.

Joseph Addison

Modesty never rages, never murmurs, never pouts; when
it is ill-treated, it pines, it beseeches, it languishes.

Richard Steele

He who speaks without modesty will find
it difficult to make his words good.

Confucius

True modesty avoids everything that is criminal;
false modesty everything that is unfashionable.

Joseph Addison

Modesty once extinguished knows not how to return.

Marcus Annaeus Seneca

Modesty seldom resides in a breast
that is not enriched with nobler virtues.

Oliver Goldsmith

Unaffected modesty is the sweetest charm of female
excellence, the richest gem in the diadem of her honor.

Noah Webster

Morality

The world has achieved brilliance without wisdom, power without conscience. Ours is a world of nuclear giants and ethical infants.

Omar Bradley

Morality isn't the light; it is only the polish on the candlestick.

Billy Sunday

A man is truly ethical only when he obeys the compulsion to help all life which he is able to assist, and shrinks from injuring anything that lives.

Albert Schweitzer

If we are to go forward, we must go back and rediscover those precious values—that all reality hinges on moral foundations and has spiritual control.

Martin Luther King, Jr.

The best way to teach morality is
to make it a habit with children.

Aristotle

In matters of style, swim with the current;
in matters of principle, stand like a rock.

Thomas Jefferson

For children to take morality seriously they
must be in the presence of adults who take
morality seriously. And with their own eyes they
must see adults take morality seriously.

William Bennett

To educate a man in mind and not in morals
is to educate a menace to society.

Theodore Roosevelt

A Bible and a newspaper in every house, a good
school in every district—all studied and
appreciated as they merit—are the principal
support of virtue, morality, and civil liberty.

Benjamin Franklin

Nonviolence

Non-violence is not a garment to be put on and
off at will. Its seat is in the heart, and it
must be an inseparable part of our being.

Mahatma Gandhi

Civilization and violence are antithetical concepts.

Martin Luther King, Jr.

The only thing necessary for the triumph
of evil is for good men to do nothing.

Edmund Burke

Today, a doctor could make a million dollars
if he could figure a way to bring a boy into
the world without a trigger finger.

Arthur Miller

Fair peace becomes men; ferocious
anger belongs to beasts.

Ovid

We must learn to live together as
brothers or perish together as fools.

Martin Luther King, Jr.

In some cases, non-violence requires
more militancy than violence.

Cesar Chavez

Nonviolence is a powerful and just weapon,
which cuts without wounding and ennobles
the man who wields it. It is a sword that heals.

Martin Luther King, Jr.

I object to violence because when it
appears to do good, the good is only
temporary; the evil it does is permanent.

Mahatma Gandhi

Social justice cannot be attained by violence.
Violence kills what it intends to create.

Pope John Paul II

Patience

Patience is not the ability to wait, but the ability to keep a good attitude while waiting.

John Dryden

The two most powerful warriors
are patience and time.

Leo Tolstoy

He that can have patience can have what he will.

Benjamin Franklin

Our patience will achieve more than our force.

Edmund Burke

Patience and perseverance have a
magical effect before which difficulties
disappear and obstacles vanish.

John Quincy Adams

Adopt the pace of nature; her secret is patience.

Ralph Waldo Emerson

Patience is the companion of wisdom.

Saint Augustine

Trees that are slow to grow bear the best fruit.

Molière

Whoever is out of patience is
out of possession of their soul.

Francis Bacon

The more patient we are, the
more understanding we become.

William Arthur Ward

We could never learn to be brave and
patient if there were only joy in the world.

Helen Keller

Patriotism

No man is entitled to the blessings of freedom
unless he be vigilant in its preservation.

Douglas MacArthur

Those who expect to reap the blessings of freedom
must, like men, undergo the fatigues of supporting it.

Thomas Paine

If we ever forget that we are One Nation
Under God, then we will be a nation gone under.

Ronald Reagan

Every post is honorable in which
a man can serve his country.

George Washington

And so, my fellow Americans, ask not what your country
can do for you; ask what you can do for your country.

John F. Kennedy

May we think of freedom, not as the right to do as we please, but as the opportunity to do what is right.

Peter Marshall

This country will not be a good place for any of us to live in unless we make it a good place for all of us to live in.

Theodore Roosevelt

We're blessed with the opportunity to stand for something—for liberty and freedom and fairness—and these are worth fighting for, worth devoting our lives to.

Ronald Reagan

Patriotism means to stand by the country. It does not mean to stand by the president or any other public official.

Theodore Roosevelt

Every good citizen makes his country's honor his own and cherishes it not only as precious but as sacred.

Andrew Jackson

Peace

You cannot shake hands with a clenched fist.

Indira Gandhi

We all live under the same sky, but
we don't all have the same horizon.

Konrad Adenauer

We must see that peace represents a sweeter music, a
cosmic melody, that is far superior to the discords of war.

Martin Luther King, Jr.

If you are yourself at peace, then there is at
least some peace in the world. Then share your
peace with everyone and everyone will be at peace.

Thomas Merton

Peace begins with a smile.

Mother Teresa

We need to devise a system within which
peace will be more rewarding than war.

Margaret Mead

If you want peace, you don't talk to
your friends, you talk to your enemy.

Desmond Tutu

Nowhere can man find a quieter or more
untroubled retreat than in his own soul.

Marcus Aurelius

Establishing lasting peace is
the work of education; all politics
can do is keep us out of war.

Maria Montessori

If we want a free and peaceful world, if we
want to make the deserts bloom and man grow
to greater dignity as a human being—we can do it.

Eleanor Roosevelt

Perseverance

Go on deserving applause, and you will be
sure to meet with it; and the way to deserve
it is to be good and to be industrious.

Thomas Jefferson

Few things are impossible to diligence and
skill . . . Great works are performed, not
by strength, but by perseverance.

Samuel Johnson

The greater the obstacle, the more glory in overcoming it.

Molière

The anvil is not afraid of the hammer.

Charles Spurgeon

Let me tell you the secret that has led me to
my goal: my strength lies solely in my tenacity.

Louis Pasteur

Many of life's failures are experienced by
people who did not realize how close they
were to success when they gave up.

Thomas Alva Edison

Every strike brings me closer to the next home run.

Babe Ruth

Constant dripping hollows out a stone.

Lucretius

The difference between perseverance and
obstinacy is that one often comes from a
strong will, and the other from a strong won't.

Henry Ward Beecher

Be like a postage stamp, stick to
something until you get there!

Josh Billings

Age wrinkles the body. Quitting wrinkles the soul.

Douglas MacArthur

Purity

The one thing worth living for
is to keep one's soul pure.

Marcus Aurelius

The real ornament of woman is her character, her purity.

Mahatma Gandhi

Purity does not mean crushing the instincts but having
the instincts as servants and not the master of the spirit.

Eric Liddell

Rare is the union of beauty and purity.

Juvenal

There is a dullness, monotony, sheer boredom
in all of life when virginity and purity are
no longer protected and prized.

Elisabeth Elliot

Purity of heart is what enables us to see.

Pope Benedict XVI

A pure hand needs no glove to cover it.

Nathaniel Hawthorne

The sun, though it passes through dirty places, remains as pure as before.

Francis Bacon

My strength is as the strength of ten because my heart is pure.

Lord Alfred Tennyson

Better keep yourself clean and bright; you are the window through which you must see the world.

George Bernard Shaw

Either we must speak as we dress, or dress as we speak. Why do we profess one thing and display another? The tongue talks of chastity, but the whole body reveals impurity.

Saint Jerome

Respect

Respect for ourselves guides our morals;
respect for others guides our manners.

Laurence Sterne

A child who is allowed to be disrespectful to his
parents, will not have true respect for anyone.

Billy Graham

I cannot conceive of a greater loss
than the loss of our self-respect.

Mahatma Gandhi

A person's a person, no matter how small.

Dr. Seuss

Being brilliant is no great feat
if you respect nothing.

Johann Wolfgang von Goethe

Give your teachers the respect they
deserve, because they are the ones who
can help you get where you need to go.

Richard Howard

It's always been a mystery to me how people can
respect themselves when they humiliate other humans.

Mahatma Gandhi

I speak to everyone the same way, whether he is
the garbage man or the president of the university.

Albert Einstein

Civilization is a method of living, an
attitude of equal respect for all men.

Jane Addams

Show me the person you honor,
for I know better by that the kind
of person you are. For you show me
what your idea of humanity is.

Thomas Carlyle

Responsibility

I think of a hero as someone who understands the degree of responsibility that comes with his freedom.

Bob Dylan

You are responsible for what you have done and people whom you have influenced.

Margaret Bourke-White

I believe that every right implies a responsibility; every opportunity, an obligation; every possession, a duty.

John D. Rockefeller, Jr.

The buck stops here.

Harry S. Truman

The price of greatness is responsibility.

Winston Churchill

Action springs not from thought,
but from a readiness for responsibility.

Dietrich Bonhoeffer

It is not only for what we do that we are held
responsible, but also for what we do not do.

Molière

I believe that we are solely responsible for our choices,
and we have to accept the consequences of every
deed, word, and thought throughout our lifetime.

Elisabeth Kübler-Ross

In the long run, we shape our lives,
and we shape ourselves. The process
never ends until we die. And the choices
we make are ultimately our own responsibility.

Eleanor Roosevelt

Though I am not always responsible
for what happens to me, I am responsible
for how I handle what happens to me.

Zig Ziglar

Self-Control

A little kingdom I possess,
Where thoughts and feelings dwell;
And very hard the task I find
Of governing it well.

Louisa May Alcott

Most powerful is he who has himself in his own power.

Marcus Annaeus Seneca

What lies in our power to do,
it lies in our power not to do.

Aristotle

Blessed is the man who, having nothing to say,
abstains from giving wordy evidence of the fact.

George Eliot

He who reigns within himself and rules his
passions, desires, and fears is more than a king.

John Milton

Man who man would be must rule the empire of himself.

Percy Bysshe Shelley

Anger is a momentary madness, so
control your passion or it will control you.

Horace

To control the mind is like trying to control a
drunken monkey that has been bitten by a scorpion.

Indian Proverb

Any fool can criticize, condemn, and complain,
but it takes character and self control
to be understanding and forgiving.

Dale Carnegie

No one is in control of your happiness but you;
therefore, you have the power to change anything
about yourself or your life that you want to change.

Barbara de Angeleis

Prudent, cautious, self-control, is wisdom's root.

Robert Burns

Self-Respect

Deal with yourself as an individual worthy of respect,
and make everyone else deal with you the same way.

Nikki Giovanni

Respect yourself and others will respect you.

Confucius

Self-respect is the root of discipline: The sense of
dignity grows with the ability to say no to oneself.

Abraham Joshua Herschel

Self-respect knows no consideration.

Mahatma Gandhi

Trust yourself. Create the kind of self that
you will be happy to live with all your life. Make
the most of yourself by fanning the tiny, inner
sparks of possibility into flames of achievement.

Golda Meir

118

If you want to be respected by others, the great thing is to respect yourself. Only by that, only by self-respect will you compel others to respect you.

Fyodor Dostoyevsky

The ultimate lesson all of us have to learn is unconditional love which includes not only others but ourselves as well.

Elizabeth Kübler-Ross

I prefer to be true to myself, even at the hazard of incurring the ridicule of others, rather than to be false, and to incur my own abhorrence.

Frederick Douglass

I have no right, by anything I do or say, to demean a human being in his own eyes. What matters is not what I think of him; it is what he thinks of himself. To undermine his self-respect is a sin.

Antoine de Saint-Exupèry

For God's sake, have some self-respect and do not run off at the mouth if your brain is out to lunch.

Anton Chekhov

Service

The only ones among you who will be really happy
are those who will have sought and found how to serve.

Albert Schweitzer

The measure of a life, after all, is
not its duration, but its donation.

Corrie ten Boom

Only a life lived for others is a life worthwhile.

Albert Einstein

Life's most persistent urgent question
is, "What are you doing for others?"

Martin Luther King, Jr.

Never believe that a few caring people can't change
the world. For, indeed, that's all who ever have.

Margaret Mead

We must restore hope to young people, help the old, be open to the future, spread love. Be poor among the poor. We need to include the excluded and preach peace.

Pope Francis

God has given us two hands—one to receive with and one to give with. We are not cisterns made for hoarding; we are channels for sharing.

Billy Graham

Unless someone like you cares a whole awful lot, nothing is going to get better. It's not.

Dr. Seuss

Remember that the happiest people are not those getting more, but those giving more.

H. Jackson Brown, Jr.

God does not ask for your ability or your inability. He asks only for your availability.

Mary Kay Ash

Speech

Speak clearly if you speak at all.
Carve every word before you let it fall.

Oliver Wendell Holmes, Sr.

A sharp tongue is the only edged tool
that grows keener with constant use.

Washington Irving

Better to remain silent and be thought a fool
than to speak out and remove all doubt.

Abraham Lincoln

Remember not only to say the right thing in the
right moment, but far more difficult, is to leave
unsaid the wrong thing in the tempting moment.

Benjamin Franklin

By words the mind is winged.

Aristophanes

Violence of the tongue is very real—
sharper than any knife.

Mother Teresa

Speak when you are angry and you will
make the best speech you will ever regret.

Ambrose Bierce

Half the world is composed of people who have
nothing to say and can't and the other half who
have nothing to say and keep on saying it.

Robert Frost

Wise men speak because they have something to
say; fools because they have to say something.

Plato

Words can do wonderful things. They can urge;
they can wheedle, whip or whine. They can
forge a fiery army out of a hundred languid men.

Gwendolyn Brooks

Spirituality

Our scientific power has outrun our spiritual power.
We have guided missiles and misguided men.

Martin Luther King, Jr.

You can preach a better sermon with
your life than with your lips.

Oliver Goldsmith

Let each one remember that he will make progress
in all spiritual things only insofar as he rids
himself of self-love, self-will and self-interest.

Saint Ignatius of Loyola

I am a little pencil in the hand of a writing
God who is sending a love letter to the world.

Mother Teresa

There never was a great soul that
did not have some divine inspiration.

Cicero

People are like stained-glass windows. They
sparkle and shine when the sun is out, but
when the darkness sets in, their true beauty
is revealed only if there is a light from within.

Elizabeth Kübler-Ross

It is not the strength of the body that
counts but the strength of the spirit.

J.R.R. Tolkein

It is this belief in a power larger than myself
and other than myself which allows me to
venture into the unknown and even the unknowable.

Maya Angelou

There is one spectacle grander than the sea,
that is the sky; there is one spectacle grander
than the sky; that is the interior of the soul.

Victor Hugo

Physical relationship divorced from
spiritual is body without soul.

Mahatma Gandhi

125

Success

I attribute my success to this: I
never gave or took any excuse.

Florence Nightingale

Every failure brings with it the
seed of an equivalent success.

Napolean Hill

The secret of success in life is for a man to
be ready for his opportunity when it comes.

Benjamin Disraeli

People rarely succeed unless they
have fun in what they are doing.

Dale Carnegie

It is hard to fail, but it is worse
never to have tried to succeed.

Theodore Roosevelt

An important key to success is self-confidence.
An important key to self-confidence is preparation.

Arthur Ashe

Success consists of getting up
just one more time than you fall.

Oliver Goldsmith

The secret of success is constancy of purpose.

Benjamin Disraeli

Success consists of going from failure to
failure to failure without loss of enthusiasm.

Winston Churchill

Nothing succeeds like success.

Alexandre Dumas

If A is a success in life, then A equals x plus y plus z.
Work is x, y is play and z is keeping your mouth shut.

Albert Einstein

Time Management

If you truly love life, don't waste time
because time is what life is made of.

Bruce Lee

Your time is limited, so don't
waste it living someone else's life.

Steve Jobs

Nine-tenths of wisdom consists of being wise in time.

Theodore Roosevelt

All we have to decide is what to do
with the time that is given to us.

J.R.R. Tolkien

Time management is really a misnomer—the
challenge is not to manage time, but to manage
ourselves. The key is not to prioritize what's on
your schedule but to schedule your priorities.

Stephen Covey

128

Procrastination is the thief of time.

Alexander Hamilton

Time is what we most want, but what we spend worse.

William Penn

Unfaithfulness in the keeping of an appointment
is an act of clear dishonesty. You may as well
borrow a person's money as his time.

Horace Mann

Better three hours too soon than one minute too late.

William Shakespeare

Either you run the day, or the day runs you.

Jim Rohn

Don't count the days;
make the days count.

Muhammad Ali

Tolerance

The highest result of education is tolerance.

Helen Keller

Think for yourself and let others
enjoy the privilege of doing so too.

Voltaire

The longer I live, the larger allowances
I make for human infirmities.

John Wesley

Intolerance is itself a form of violence and an
obstacle to the growth of a true democratic spirit.

Mahatma Gandhi

What I cannot love, I overlook.

Anäis Nin

Discord is the great ill of mankind; and
tolerance is the only remedy for it.

Voltaire

Nothing in life is to be feared;
it is only to be understood.

Marie Curie

Anger and intolerance are the
enemies of correct understanding.

Mahatma Gandhi

Tolerance implies no lack of commitment
to one's own beliefs. Rather it condemns
the oppression or persecution of others.

John F. Kennedy

The responsibility of tolerance lies
with those who have the wider vision.

George Eliot

Trust

Self-trust is the first secret of success.

Ralph Waldo Emerson

Trust is the glue of life. It's the most essential
ingredient in effective communication. It's the
foundational principle that holds all relationships.

Stephen Covey

Few delights can equal the mere presence
of one whom we trust utterly.

George MacDonald

Woe to man whose heart has not learned while
young to hope, to love—and to put its trust in life.

Joseph Conrad

Although the life of a person is in a land full of
thorns and weeds, there's always a space in which
the good seed can grow. You have to trust God.

Pope Francis

Anyone who doesn't take truth seriously in small matters cannot be trusted in large ones either.

Albert Einstein

Do not trust all men, but trust men of worth; the former course is silly, the latter a mark of prudence.

Democritus

Trust should be the basis for all our moral training.

Robert Baden-Powell

Trust, but verify.

Ronald Reagan

All I have seen teaches me to trust the Creator for all I have not seen.

Ralph Waldo Emerson

Never be afraid to trust an unknown future to a known God.

Corrie ten Boom

Truth

Truth is tough. It will not break, like a bubble, at a touch; nay, you may kick it about all day like a football, and it will be round and full at evening.

Oliver Wendell Holmes, Sr.

Don't worry about being effective. Just concentrate on being faithful to the truth.

Dorothy Day

A truth that's told with bad intent
beats all the lies you can invent.

William Blake

A lie stands on one leg, the truth on two.

Benjamin Franklin

Man will occasionally stumble over the truth, but most of the time he will pick himself up and continue on.

Winston Churchill

The false can never grow into
truth by growing into power.

Rabindranath Tagore

An error does not become truth by reason
of multiplied propaganda, nor does truth
become error because nobody sees it.

Mahatma Gandhi

The further a society drifts from the truth,
the more it will hate those that speak it.

George Orwell

I believe that unarmed truth and unconditional
love will have the final word in reality.

Martin Luther King, Jr.

Truth is by nature self-evident; as soon
as you remove the cobwebs of ignorance
that surround it, it shines clear.

Mahatma Gandhi

Virtue

A good conscience is a continual feast.

Sir Francis Bacon

Consider your origins: you were not born to live
like brutes but to follow virtue and knowledge.

Dante

And virtue, though in rags, will warm me.

John Dryden

Virtue is like a rich stone, best plain set.

Sir Francis Bacon

Virtue has a veil, vice a mask.

Victor Hugo

All the gold, which is under or upon the earth
is not enough to give in exchange for virtue.

Plato

Few men have virtue to withstand the highest bidder.

George Washington

There is nothing meritorious but virtue and friendship.

Alexander Pope

Love is the virtue of the heart, sincerity is the virtue of the mind. Decision is the virtue of the will, courage is the virtue of the spirit.

Frank Lloyd Wright

The superior man thinks always of virtue; the common man thinks of comfort.

Confucius

That which is inherent in men is his virtue.

Mahatma Gandhi

Virtue is a wealth, and all the other good things that a man can have come from virtue.

Socrates

Wisdom

The fool wonders, the wise man asks.

Benjamin Disraeli

A wise man will make more opportunities than he finds.

Francis Bacon

It is characteristic of wisdom not to do desperate things.

Henry David Thoreau

Knowledge comes, but wisdom lingers.

Lord Alfred Tennyson

We need to haunt the halls of history
and listen anew to the ancestors' wisdom.

Maya Angelou

Wisdom comes alone through suffering.

Aeschylus

A wise man will desire no more than
what he may get justly, use soberly,
distribute cheerfully, and leave contently.

Benjamin Franklin

A man should never be ashamed to own he has
been in the wrong, which is but saying, in other
words, that he is wiser today than he was yesterday.

Alexander Pope

A fool thinks himself to be wise, but a
wise man knows himself to be a fool.

William Shakespeare

The art of being wise is the art
of knowing what to overlook.

William James

I look forward to a future in which our country will
match its military strength with our moral restraint,
its wealth with our wisdom, its power with our purpose.

John F. Kennedy

Work

The only place where success comes
before work is in the dictionary.

Vidal Sassoon

The most practical, beautiful, workable
philosophy in the world won't work—if you won't.

Zig Ziglar

The highest reward for man's toil is not what
he gets for it, but what he becomes by it.

John Ruskin

All labor that uplifts humanity has dignity and importance
and should be undertaken with painstaking excellence.

Martin Luther King, Jr.

A life of leisure and a life of laziness are two things.
There will be sleeping enough in the grave.

Benjamin Franklin

You can't wring your hands and roll
up your sleeves at the same time.

Pat Schroeder

It is the quality of our work, which
will please God and not the quantity.

Mahatma Gandhi

The world is full of willing people, some
willing to work, the rest willing to let them.

Robert Frost

When you play, play hard; when you work, don't play at all.

Theodore Roosevelt

Labor disgraces no man. Unfortunately, you
occasionally find men who disgrace labor.

Ulysses S. Grant

Choose a job you love, and you will
never have to work a day in your life.

Confucius

Glossary

A

John Quincy Adams: (1767-1848) American statesman and sixth President of the United States

Joseph Addison: (1672-1719) British essayist and politician remembered for his publication *The Spectator*

Konrad Adenauer: (1876-1967) German statesman and post World War II Chancellor of West Germany

Aeschylus: (525 B.C.-456 B.C.) Greek tragedian who wrote 90 plays; known as the founder of Greek tragedy; "Prometheus Unbound"

Aesop: (620-564 B.C.) Ancient Greek storyteller; *Aesop's Fables*

Madeline Albright: (1937--) First female U.S. Secretary of State who also served as ambassador to the United Nations

Louisa May Alcott: (1832-1888) American novelist; *Little Women*

Alexander the Great: (356 B.C.-323 B.C.) Alexander III of Macedon was the Macedonian king who united Greece, led the Corinthian League, and conquered the Persian Empire

Muhammad Ali: (1942-2016) Born Cassius Clay, American boxing champion who became the first heavyweight to win the championship title four times

James Lane Allen: (1849-1925) American novelist and short story writer; *A Kentucky Cardinal*

Saint Ambrose: (340-397 Italian Bishop of Milan and one of the most influential ecclesiastical figures of the fourth century

Maya Angelou: (1928-2014) American author, poet, dancer, actress, and singer; *I Know Why the Caged Bird Sings*

Susan B. Anthony: (1820-1906) American social reformer and feminist who played a pivotal role in the women's suffrage movement

Aristotle: (384-322 B.C.) Greek philosopher, educator, and scientist who was a student of the great philosopher Plato

George Arnold: (1834-1865) U.S. author and poet who became a regular contributor to the popular magazine *Vanity Fair*

Mary Kay Ash: (1918-2001) American businesswoman and founder of Mary Kay Cosmetics

Arthur Ashe: (1943-1993) American World No. 1 professional tennis player who won three Grand Slam titles

Saint Thomas Aquinas: (1225-1274) Italian Dominican friar and Catholic priest

Saint Augustine: (354-430 A.D.) Roman Christian leader whose writings influenced the development of Western Christianity and philosophy

Marcus Aurelius: (121 to 180 A.D.) Roman emperor and Stoic philosopher

B

Sir Francis Bacon: (1561-1626) British philosopher, statesman, and scientist who was one of the earliest supporters of using experiments and observation to learn more about nature

Robert Baden-Powell: (1857-1941) Founder of the Boy Scouts

Honore de Balzac: (1799-1850) French novelist and playwright

Clara Barton: (1821-1912) U.S. nurse and founder of the American Red Cross

Simone de Beauvoir: (1908-1986) French writer, philosopher, and feminist; *The Second Sex*

Henry Ward Beecher: (1813-1887) American Congregationalist clergy, social reformer, speaker, and abolitionist

Pope Benedict XVI: (1927--) The 265th Pope of the Roman Catholic Church

Stephen Vincent Benet: (1898-1943) U.S. author known for his poetry and short stories that reflect his love of American history

William Bennett: (1943--) American conservative pundit, politician, and political theorist who served as Secretary of Education under President Reagan

Mary McLeod Bethune: (1875-1955) U.S. educator who established Bethune-Cookman College in Florida, and served as advisor to several U.S. presidents

Ambrose Bierce: (1842-1914) American author known for his realistic war stories as well as his humor; "An Occurrence at Owl Creek Bridge"

Josh Billings: (1818-1885) A 19th century American humorist

Tony Blair: (1953--) British Labor Party politician and Prime Minister of the United Kingdom from 1997-2007

William Blake: (1757-1827) British painter, poet and printmaker of the Romantic Age who used symbolism and unusual images

Dietrich Bonhoeffer: (1906-1945) German Lutheran pastor, theologian, and anti-Nazi dissident; *The Cost of Discipleship*

Corrie ten Boom: (1892-1983) Dutch Christian who helped many Jews escape the Nazi Holocaust during World War II; *The Hiding Place*

E.M. Bounds: (1835-1913) Edward McKendree Bounds was an American attorney, clergy, and author of eleven books, mostly about prayer

Margaret Bourke-White: (1904-1971) American photojournalist who was the first American female war photojournalist

Ray Bradbury: (1920-2012) American fantasy, science fiction, horror and mystery fiction author; *Fahrenheit 451* and *The Martian Chronicles*

Bill Bradley: (1943--) American Hall of Fame basketball player, Rhodes scholar, and former three-term Democratic Senator from New Jersey

Omar Bradley: (1893-1981) American military general and first Chairman of the Joint Chiefs of Staff

Sarah Ban Breathnach: (1947--) American writer *(Simple Abundance)*

Charlotte Bronte: (1816-1855) English novelist and poet; *Jane Eyre*

Gwendolyn Brooks: (1917-2000) American poet and teacher; first African-American woman to win a Pulitzer Price; *Annie Allen*

H. Jackson Brown, Jr.: (1940--) American author best known for *Life's Little Instruction Book*

Elizabeth Barrett Browning: (1806-1861) One of the most prominent English poets of the Victorian era; "Sonnets from the Portuguese"

Robert Browning: (1812-1889) English poet and playwright; famous for dramatic monologues like "My Last Duchess"

William Jennings Bryan: (1860-1925) American journalist and politician; U.S. House of Representative and U.S. Secretary of State under Woodrow Wilson

Pearl S. Buck: (1892-1973) American writer and novelist; *The Good Earth* won the Pulitzer Prize in 1932; Buck won the Nobel Prize in Literature in 1938

Edmund Burke: (1729-1797) British statesman during the American Revolution who urged the British government to grant the Colonists more rights to keep them part of the nation

Robert Burns: (1759-1796) Scottish poet and lyricist; national poet of Scotland; "Auld Lang Syne"

Lord Byron: (1788-1824) George Gordon Byron was an English poet and leading figure in the Romantic movement; *Don Juan* and *Childe Harold's Pilgrimage*

C

Thomas Carlyle: (1795-1881) Scottish author, philosopher, and historian during the Victorian era; "Courage, Language and Words"

Amy Carmichael: (1867-1951) Protestant Christian missionary in India for fifty-five years; she founded an orphanage in Dohnavur; *If*

Dale Carnegie: (1888-1955) American educator who developed the famous courses in self-improvement; *How to Win Friends and Influence People*

Rosalynn Carter: (1927--) First Lady of the United States as the wife of the 39th President of the United States, Jimmy Carter

Miguel de Cervantes: (1547-1616) The greatest writer in the Spanish language; *Don Quixote*

William Henry Channing: (1810-1884) American Unitarian clergyman and writer

Cesar Chavez: (1927-1993) American farm worker, labor leader, and civil rights activist who co-founded the United Farm Workers Union and organized California grape pickers in 1962

Anton Chekhov: (1860-1904) Russian playwright and short story writer; *The Cherry Orchard*

G.K. Chesterton: (1874-1936) English writer, orator, critic and Christian apologist; *Heretics*

Winston Churchill: (1874-1965) British statesman and prime minister during World War II, army officer, historian, and writer; won Nobel Prize for Literature in 1953

Marcus Tullius Cicero: (106 B.C.-43 B.C.) Roman orator, poet and statesman who was killed by the Second Triumvirate because he opposed their rule

Henry Clay: (1777-1852) U.S. Senator from Kentucky known as the Great Compromiser because he often helped to settle conflicts about slavery between Northern and Southern states

Saint Clement of Alexandria: (150-215) Christian theologian who taught at the Catechetical School of Alexandria; *The Trilogy*

Grover Cleveland: (1837-1908) The 22nd and 24th President of the United States

Samuel Taylor Coleridge: (1772-1834) English poet, literary critic and philosopher who, with William Wordsworth, founded the Romantic Movement in England; "The Rime of the Ancient Mariner"

Confucius: (551 B.C.-479 B.C.) Chinese teacher and philosopher whose ideas influenced culture and ethics in China, Japan, Korea, and Vietnam

Joseph Conrad: (1857-1924) English novelist; *Heart of Darkness*

Captain James Cook (1728-1779) British explorer, navigator, cartographer and captain in the Royal Navy

Calvin Coolidge: (1872-1933) The 30th President of the United States who led the country during the 1920s

Sean Covey: (1964--) American motivational speaker and author of the Seven Habits series.

Stephen Covey: (1932-2012) American educator, author, businessman, and keynote speaker; *The Seven Habits of Highly Effective People*

Davy Crockett: (1786-1836) American folk hero, frontiersman, soldier, and politician who served in the Tennessee legislature and U.S. Senate; he died in the battle of the Alamo in Texas

Marie Curie: (1867-1934) Polish and native French physician and chemist who pioneered research in radioactivity; one of the few scientists to win a Nobel Price for both Chemistry and Physics

D

Ronald Dahl: (1916-1990) British author known for eerie adult stories and funny novels for children; *James and the Giant Peach, Charlie and the Chocolate Factory*

Dante: (1265-1321) First name Alighieri but known as Dante; Italian poet and writer; *The Divine Comedy*

Adelle Davis: (1896-1953) Nutritionist and writer

Dorothy Day: (1897-1980) American social reformer and cofounder of the Catholic Worker Movement

Barbara de Angelis: (1951--) American relationship consultant, teacher, and author; *Soul Shifts*

Charles de Gaulle: (1890-1970) French general, resistant writer, and statesman; 18th President of France

Democritus: (460-370 B.C.) Influential Ancient Greek pre-Socratic philosopher; formulated the atomic theory of the universe

John Dewey: (1859-1952) American philosopher and educator; created the Dewey Decimal System

Diana, Princess of Wales: (1981-1996) Title of Lady Diana Frances Spencer, wife of Charles, Prince of Wales

Charles Dickens: (1812-1870) British writer known for his tales of Victorian life; *David Copperfield*

Emily Dickinson: (1830-1886) Popular American poet who wrote more than 1,700 poems but published few during her lifetime; "Animals"; "Faith and Hope"

Walt Disney: (1901-1966) American animator and motion picture executive who created Mickey Mouse and Donald Duck and whose full-length animated features include *Snow White and the Seven Dwarfs.*

Benjamin Disraeli: (1804-1881) Jewish British prime minister and novelist

Dorothea Dix: (1802-1887) American activist on behalf of the indigent insane; created first generation of American mental asylums

John Donne: (1572-1631) English cleric and poet; *"Death Be Not Proud"*

Fyodor Dostoyevsky: (1821-1881) Russian author; *Crime and Punishment*

Frederick Douglass: (1817-1895) U.S. and Canadian journalist and civil rights leader who campaigned for the rights of African Americans

John Dryden: (1631-1700) English writer whose works include critical essays, dramas, and poems

Alexander Dumas: (1802-1870) French writer whose famous romantic novels include *The Count of Monte Cristo* and *The Three Musketeers*

Bob Dylan: (1941--) American singer, songwriter, and writer, who won the Nobel Prize in Literature in 2016; "Blowin' in the Wind"

E

Amelia Earhart: (1897-1937) American aviation pioneer who was the first female aviator to fly solo across the Atlantic Ocean; she later disappeared over the Pacific Ocean

Meister Eckhart: (1260-1327) German theologian regarded as the founder of mysticism in Germany

Thomas Alva Edison: (1847-1931) American inventor who patented 1,093 inventions, among them the phonograph in 1878 and an incandescent lamp in 1879

Jonathan Edwards: (1703-1758) American theologian whose works stimulated the Great Awakening, a period of renewed American interest in religion

Albert Einstein: (1879-1955) German-born scientist whose theories of relativity won a 1921 Nobel Prize; he was also a champion of human rights and peace

Dwight D. Eisenhower: (1890-1969) American General and 34th President of the United States

George Eliot: (1819-1880) Pen name of Mary Ann Evans, a British writer; *Middlemarch, Silas Marner*

Elisabeth Elliot: (1926-2015) Christian author and speaker; her husband, Jim Elliot, was martyred in Ecuador

Ralph Waldo Emerson: (1803-1882) American philosopher, writer, and minister who believed in being true to oneself

Mary Engelbreit: (1952--) Graphic artist and children's book illustrator

Epictetus: (55-135 A.D.) Phrygian-born Stoic philosopher who believed that one should act in life as one would at a banquet, by taking a polite portion of all that is offered

Euripides: (485-406 B.C.) Greek dramatist whose surviving works include *Medea* and *The Trojan Women*

Antoine de Saint Exupéry: (1900-1944) French aristocrat, writer, poet, dentist, and pioneering aviator who perceived God in all of nature; *The Little Prince*

F

William Faulkner: (1897-1962) American writer and Nobel Prize laureate from Oxford, Mississippi; *The Sound and the Fury; The Reivers*

Henry Fielding: (1707-1754) English novelist and dramatist known for his satire; *Tom Jones*

Harrison Ford: (1942--) American film actor and producer; *Star Wars*

Henry Ford: (1863-1947) American industrialist and founder of the Ford Motor Company; he developed the assembly line technique of mass production

E. M. Forster: (1879-1970) English novelist, short story writer, essayist and librettist; nominated for the Nobel Prize in Literature thirteen times

Pope Francis: (1936--) The first Jesuit pope and the first pope from the Americas; sought to reform the Vatican and the Catholic church; stressed the importance of modesty, humility, and concern for the poor.

Anne Frank: (1929-1945) German Jewish diarist and writer with an optimistic spirit and faith during the Holocaust of World War II; *The Diary of Anne Frank*

Viktor Frankl: (1905-1997) Austrian neurologist, psychiatrist, and Holocaust survivor who wrote *Man's Search for Meaning*

Benjamin Franklin: (1706-1790) American statesman, writer, and printer who published *Poor Richard's Almanac;* he invented bifocal eyeglasses and the Franklin stove

Erich Fromm: (1900-1980) German-born American psychoanalyst whose works include *Escape from Freedom*

Robert Frost: (1874-1963) Most popular American poet of his time whose works are often set in rural New England; in 1960 Congress gave Frost a gold medal for his poetic contribution

Thomas Fuller: (1608-1661) English churchman and historian; *Worthies of England*

John Galsworthy: (1867-1933) English novelist and playwright who won a Nobel Prize in Literature in 1932; *The Forsythe Saga*

Indira Gandhi: (1917-1984) Indian politician and first female prime minister of India, who was assassinated in 1984 by two of her bodyguards; principle figurehead of the Indian independence movement; taught a philosophy of non-violence and peaceful protest

Mahatma Gandhi: (1869-1948) Mohandas Mahatma was called Mohandas, which means "Great Soul"; Indian nationalist leader of the nonviolent effort to free India from British rule

Elizabeth George: (1949--) American author of more than 70 books; national speaker; *A Devotional Journey Through God's Word*

Kahlil Gibran: (1883-1931) Syrian-born U.S. author who wrote in Arabic and English; *The Prophet*

Nikki Giovanni (1943--) U.S. poet, essayist, and author of children's books that focus on the African American woman; "Experience"

Johann Wolfgang von Goethe: (1749-1832) German writer, scientist, and court official best known for his dramatic poem "Faust"

Samuel Goldwyn: (1882-1974) Jewish Polish American film producer and owner of motion picture studios in Hollywood

Billy Graham: (1918--) American religious leader and writer famous for his world-wide evangelical tours

Ulysses S. Grant: (1822-1885) The 18th President of the United States and Commanding General of the U.S. Army; he
led the Union Army to victory over the Confederacy in the American Civil War

Marcus Gravey: (1887-1940) Jamaican political leader, publisher, journalist, entrepreneur, and orator

Horace Greeley: (1811-1872) Editor of the *New-York Tribune,* among the great newspapers of its time

Lee Greenwood: (1942--) American country music artist; most famous for "God Bless the U.S.A."

Wayne Gretzky: (1961--) Canadian former professional ice hockey player and former head coach

Edgar A. Guest: (1881-1959) U.S. poet and journalist known as the People's Poet; "Home"

H

Nathan Hale: (1755-1776) Soldier for the Continental Army during the American Revolutionary War; he was captured by the British and executed

Hammurabi: (died 1750 B.C.) First King of the First Babylonian Dynasty known for the Code of Hammurabi, one of the earliest codes of law

Nathaniel Hawthorne: (1804-1864) American novelist and short story writer; *The Scarlett Letter*

Rutherford B. Hayes: (1822-1893) The 19th President of the United States

William Hazlitt: (1778-1830) British essayist whose works include "The Spirit of the Age"

Patrick Henry: (1736-1799) American attorney, planter, politician, and orator during work for independence in Virginia in the 1770s

Katharine Hepburn: (1907-2003) Belgian-born American actress whose films include "Breakfast at Tiffany's

George Herbert: (1593-1633) Welsh-born English metaphysical poet, orator, and Anglican priest

Abraham Joshua Herschel: (1907-1972) Polish-born American rabbi and a leading Jewish theologian of the 20th century

Napoleon Hill: (1883-1970) American author of personal success literature; *Think and Grow Rich* was one of the top selling books of all times

Conrad Hilton: (1887-1979) American hotelier and founder of the Hilton Hotels

Hippocrates: (460-370 B.C.) Ancient Greek physician of the Age of Pericles; known as the "Father of Western Medicine"

Oliver Wendell Holmes, Sr.: (1809-1894) American jurist; associate justice of the U.S. Supreme Court

Homer: (8th Century) Greek epic poet and author of the *Iliad* and the *Odyssey*

Horace: (65 B.C.-8 B.C.) Quintius Horatius Fiaccus was the leading Roman lyric poet during the time of Augustus (also known as Octavian); *Odes*

Richard Howard: (1929--) American poet, literary critic, essayist, teacher, and translator

Langston Hughes: (1902-1967) American poet and author of more than 50 books; innovator of jazz poetry and leader of the Harlem Renaissance

Victor Hugo: (1802-1885) French writer; *The Hunchback of Notre Dame; Les Misérables*

Aldous Huxley: (1894-1963) British writer who believed that science was destroying people's values; *Brave New World*

I

Lee Iacocca: (1924--) American automobile executive best known for developing Ford Mustang and Pinto cars and for reviving the Chrysler Corporation

Henrik Ibsen: (1828-1906) Major 19th century Norwegian playwright, theater director, and poet; *A Doll's House*

Saint Ignatius of Loyola: (1491-1556) Spanish soldier and ecclesiastic who founded the Jesuits

Washington Irving: (1783-1859) American writer whose stories drew on the cultural traditions of the Dutch and other European settlers of New York State; "The Legend of Sleepy Hollow" and "Rip Van Winkle"

J

Andrew Jackson: (1767-1845) Known as "Old Hickory", Jackson was born in Tennessee; he became the 7th President of the United States

William James: (1842-1910) American philosopher and psychologist who was also trained as a physician; "Father of American Psychology"

Thomas Jefferson: (1743-1826) One of America's founding fathers who helped draft the Declaration of Independence; third U.S. President

Saint Jerome: (347-420 A.D.) Priest, theologian and historian best known for his translation of the Bible into Latin (known as the Vulgate)

Steve Jobs: (1955-2011) American entrepreneur and inventor; founder of Apple Company

Samuel Johnson: (1709-1784) British writer, critic and lexicographer who wrote the *Dictionary of the English Language*

Ben Jonson: (1572-1637) English poet, literary critic, and playwright; *Volpone*

Carl Jung: (1875-1961) Swiss psychiatrist and founder of analytical psychology

Juvenal: (55-130 A.D.) Roman author who originated the genre of Roman satire

K

John Keats: (1795-1821) British poet whose works include "Ode on a Grecian Urn" and "Endymion"

Garrison Keillor: (1942--) American author, storyteller, humorist, and radio personality who hosted "A Prairie Home Companion"

Helen Keller: (1880-1968) American writer who lectured on behalf of sightless people

John F. Kennedy: (1917-1963) American politician and 35th President of the United States until he was assassinated in November, 1963

Martin Luther King, Jr.: (1929-1968) American minister and civil rights leader; he won the 1964 Nobel Peace Prize before being assassinated; he inspired millions of people of all races to aspire for a more equal and just society

Rudyard Kipling: (1865-1936) British writer who was born in India and who wrote *The Jungle Book*, in 1907, he became the first English author to win the Nobel Prize in Literature

Elisabeth Kübler-Ross: (1926-2004) Swiss-American psychiatrist, a pioneer in near-death studies; *On Death and Dying*

Harold Kushner: (1935--) American rabbi and author aligned with Conservative Judaism; *When Bad Things Happen to Good People*

L

Bruce Lee: (1940—1973) Hong Kong American martial artist, Hong Kong action film actor, martial arts instructor and filmmaker

Madeleine L'Engle: (1918-2007) American writer known for her young adult fiction; she won the Newbery Award in 1963 for her science fiction classic *A Wrinkle in Time*

C.S. Lewis: (1898-1963) British writer, critic, and Christian apologist; *The Screwtape Letters* and *The Chronicles of Narnia*

Eric Liddell: (1902-1945) Won a gold medal in the 1924 Paris Olympics; became famous for turning down the opportunity to compete on a Sunday; became a missionary

Abraham Lincoln: (1809-1865) The 16th President of the United States, who led the Union during the Civil War and emancipated slaves in the South

Walter Lippmann: (1889-1974) American writer, reporter, and political commentator who was the first to introduce the idea of the Cold War

John Locke: (1632-1704) British philosopher whose *Essays Concerning Human Understanding* influenced Thomas Jefferson and others about empiricism

Vince Lombardi: (1913-1970) American football player, coach, and executive; coached Green Bay Packers to numerous championships; voted into the Pro Football Hall of Fame in 1971

Henry Wadsworth Longfellow: (1807-1882) American poet and educator; *The Song of Hiawatha* and *Paul Revere's Ride*

Richard Lovelace: (1617-1657) English cavalier poet who fought for the King during the English Civil War

James Russell Lowell: (1857-1861) American poet and diplomat who edited the *Atlantic Monthly*

Lucretius: (99 B.C.-55 B.C.) Roman poet and philosopher

Martin Luther: (1483-1546) German theologian and leader of the Protestant Reformation

M

Douglas MacArthur: (1880-1964) American five-star general who led troops in both World War I and World War II

George MacDonald: (1824-1905) Scottish novelist and poet Scottish author, poet, and Christian minister; pioneered fantasy writing; *The Princess and the Goblin*

Nicolò Machiavelli: (1469-1527) Italian historian, politician, diplomat, philosopher, humanist, and writer based in Florence during the Renaissance; "The Prince"

John Madden: (1936--) Former American football player; NFL commentator; Pro Football Hall of Famer; and Super Bowl-winning coach with the Oakland Raiders

Nelson Mandela: (1918-2013) South African politician and anti-apartheid revolutionary; after 20 years in jail, he became the first President of democratic South Africa

Horace Mann: (1796-1859) American politician and educator who fought for educational reforms; "Father of the Common School Movement"

Christopher Marlowe: (1564-1593) English playwright, poet, and translator

Peter Marshall: (1902-1949) Scottish-born American Presbyterian clergyman and theologian

John C. Maxwell: (1947--) Leadership expert, minister, speaker, and author

Dr. Phil McGraw: (1950--) American television personality, author, psychologist, and host of the "Dr. Phil" television show

Margaret Mead: (1901-1978) American anthropologist and writer; *Coming of Age in Somoa*

Golda Meir: (1898-1978) Israeli teacher, politician, and 4th Prime Minister of Israel

Herman Melville: (1819-1891) U.S. author who spent part of his childhood at sea as a cabin boy and part of his adulthood as a seaman aboard whaling ships; *Moby Dick*

Thomas Merton: (1915-1968) American Catholic writer and Trappist monk of the Abbey of Gesthsemani, Kentucky: *The Seven Storey Mountain*

Michelangelo: (1475-1564) Italian sculptor, painter, architect, poet, and engineer of the High Renaissance period; famous for fresco he painted on the ceiling of the Sistine Chapel in the Vatican; "David"

John Stuart Mill: (1806-1873) British philosopher, political scientist, and civil servant

Edna St. Vincent Millay: (1892-1950) American lyrical poet and playwright; won Pulitzer Prize in Poetry in 1923

Arthur Miller: (1915-2005) American playwright, essayist, and prominent figure in 20th century American theater; won Pulitzer Prize for his play *Death of a Salesman, The Crucible*

Molière: (1622-1673) French playwright and actor; *The Misanthrope*

Lady Mary Wortley Montagu: (1689-1762) English aristocrat and writer; remembered for her letters from Turkey as the wife to British ambassador

Michel de Montaigne: (1533-1592) One of the most significant philosophers of the French Renaissance; known for popularizing the essay as a literary genre; *Essais*

Maria Montessori: (1870-1952) Italian physician and educator; founded the philosophy of education that bears her name

James Montgomery: (1949--) American blues musician and bandleader of The James Montgomery Blues Band

Dwight L. Moody: (1837-1899) American evangelist and preacher who founded the Moody Church and the Moody Bible Institute

Christopher Morley: (1890-1957) American journalist, novelist, essayist, and poet

John Muir: (1838-1914) Scottish-born U.S. naturalist, author, and founder of The Sierra Club

N

John Naisbitt: (1929--) American author and public speaker in the area of future studies; *Megatrends*

Ogden Nash: (1902-1971) American poet known for his light verse; "Animals"

Florence Nightingale: (1820-1910) English nurse, writer, and statistician who came into prominence during the Crimean War for her pioneering work in nursing

Anaïs Nin: (1903-1977) French-American diarist

O

Jacqueline Kennedy Onassis: (1929-1994) First Lady when she was the wife of the 35th President of the U.S., John F. Kennedy

James Oppenheim: (1882-1932) American poet, novelist, and editor

George Orwell: (1903-1950) English novelist, essayist, journalist, and critic who wrote the novel *1984*; he warned about the dangers of totalitarianism

Ovid: (43 B.C.-17/18 A.D.) Popular name for Publius Ovidius Naso; Roman poet living during the reign of Augustus, and a contemporary of Virgil and Horace; *Metamorphosis*

Jesse Owens: (1913-1980) Won four gold medals at Hitler's 1936 Olympics in Berlin, which helped to puncture the Nazi ideology of Aryan Supremacy

P

Thomas Paine: (1737-1809) English-American political activist, philosopher, and revolutionary; wrote influential pamphlets arguing for independence for the U.S.; "Common Sense"

Louis Pasteur: (1822-1895) French chemist and microbiologist; famous for his principles of vaccination and pasteurization

George S. Patton: (1885-1945) Famous U.S. Army general during World War II

Pope John Paul II: (1920-2005) Roman Catholic priest, bishop, and cardinal who eventually rose to become Pope

Normal Vincent Peale: (1898-1993) Minister and author; progenitor of "positive thinking"; *The Power of Positive Thinking*

William Penn: (1644-1718) American clergy who founded the Pennsylvania Colony

James Cash Penney: (1875-1971) American businessman and entrepreneur who, in 1902, founded the J.C. Penney stores

Pablo Picasso: (1881-1973) Spanish painter, sculptor, printmaker, ceramicist, stage designer, poet and playwright

Plato: (428-348 B.C.) Greek philosopher, mathematician, and founder of the Academy in Athens; *The Republic*

Plutarch: (46-120 A.D.) Greek historian, biographer, and essayist; best known for *Parallel Lives* and *Morabia*

Alexander Pope: (1688-1744) English poet best known for his satirical work, "The Rape of the Lock" and for his translation of Homer

Emily Post: (1872-1960) American author famous for writing about etiquette

R

Nancy Reagan: (1921-2016) American actress and the wife of the 40th President of the U.S., Ronald Reagan

Ronald Reagan: (1911-2004) 40th President of the United States; former governor of California and actor

Rainer Maria Rilke: (1875-1926) A Bohemian-Austrian poet and novelist; *The Book of Hours*

Tony Robbins: (1960--) American motivational speaker, personal, finance instructor, life coach and self-help author; *Unlimited Power*

Jackie Robinson: (1919-1972) First black player in major league baseball in 1947; career batting average .311; inducted into Baseball Hall of Fame in 1962

John D. Rockefeller, Jr.: (1839-1937) American business magnate and philanthropist; co-founder of Standard Oil Company

Will Rogers: (1879-1935) Cherokee cowboy, vaudeville performer, humorist, and newspaper columnist

Jim Rohn: (1930-2009) American entrepreneur, author, and motivational speaker; *Five Major Pieces to the Life Puzzle*

Eleanor Roosevelt: (1884-1962) American politician, diplomat, activist, and humanitarian; First Lady of the United States (married to Franklin D. Roosevelt); helped draft United Nations Declaration of Human Rights

Franklin Delano Roosevelt: (1882-1945) American statesman and political leader; 32nd President of the United States

Theodore Roosevelt: (1858-1919) American statesman, author, explorer, naturalist, and historian; 26th President of the United States after President William McKinley was assassinated

J.K. Rowling: (1965--) English writer; known for the Harry Potter fantasy series

John Ruskin: (1819-1900) Leading English art critic of the Victorian era, social thinker, and philanthropist

Bertrand Russell: (1872-1970) British philosopher, mathematician, historian, writer, social critic, and political activist

Babe Ruth: (1895-1948) George Herman Ruth was an American Major League Baseball legend who hit 714 homeruns in his 22 seasons

Samuel Rutherford: (1600-1661) Scottish Presbyterian pastor, theologian, and author

S

Vidal Sassoon: (1928-2012) British hairdresser, businessman, and philanthropist

Arthur Schopenhauer: (1788-1860) German philosopher best known for his book *The World as Will and Representation*

Pat Schroeder: (1940--) U.S. politician who served in Congress representing the state of Colorado; she advocated women's rights, civil rights, and gun control

Robert Schuller: (1926-2015) American Christian televangelist, motivational speaker, author and host of *Hour of Power*; *If It's Going to Be, It's Up to Me*

Charles Schulz: (1922-2000) American cartoonist who created the comic strip *Peanuts*, which starred Charlie Brown, Snoopy, Linus, and Lucy

Albert Schweitzer: (1875-1960) German physician, theologian, organist, and medical missionary to Africa; *Reverence for Life*

Marcus Annaeus Seneca: (4 B.C.-65 A.D.) Seneca the Younger was a Roman Stoic philosopher, statesman, and dramatist of the Silver Age of Latin literature; "Education and Learning"

Dr. Seuss: (1904-1991) Theodor Seuss Geisel was an American writer and cartoonist; *The Cat in the Hat*

William Shakespeare: (1564-1616) English poet, and playwright who is one of the most read and most quoted authors in the world; *Hamlet, Macbeth*

George Bernard Shaw: (1856-1950) Irish playwright and co-founder of the London School of Economics; *Pygmalian*

Percy Bysshe Shelley: (1792-1822) One of the major Romantic poets, regarded as among the finest lyric poets in the English language; "Prometheus Unbound"

Philip Sidney: (1554-1586) English poet, courtier, scholar and soldier and a prominent figure of the Elizabethan age; "Astrophel and Stella"

Gary Smalley: (1940-2016) Family counselor and author of books on family relationships from a Christian perspective

Margaret Chase Smith: (1897-1995) American politician; U.S. Representative and Congresswoman from Maine

Socrates: (469-399 B.C.) Classical Greek philosopher and teacher of Plato, a founder of Western philosophy; his method of self-enquiry laid the foundations of Western Philosophic thought

Alexander Solzhenitsyn: (1918-2008) Russian novelist, historian, and short story writer who criticized the Soviet Union's totalitarianism and its Gulag forced labor camp system; he won the 1970 Nobel Prize in Literature; *One Day in the Life of Ivan Denisovich; Cancer Ward*

Sophocles: (497/6 B.C.-406/B.C.) One of three ancient Greek tragedians whose plays have survived; *Antigone; Oedipus the King*

Herbert Spencer: (1820-1903) English philosopher, biologist, anthropologist, sociologist, and political theorist

Charles Spurgeon: (1834-1892) British preacher known as the "Prince of Preachers"

Sir Richard Steele: (1672-1729) Irish writer and politician

Laurence Sterne: (1713-1768)) Anglo-Irish novelist; Anglican clergyman; *The Life and Opinions of Tristram Shandy*

Adlai Stevenson: (1834-1914) American politician; 23rd Vice President of the United States

Harriett Beecher Stowe: (1811-1896) American abolitionist and author; *Uncle Tom's Cabin*

Billy Sunday: (1862-1935) American athlete in baseball's National League who became an influential evangelist

Jonathan Swift: (1667-1745) Irish-born English satirist, essayist, political pamphleteer, poet, cleric, and author of *Gulliver's Travels*

T

Rabindranath Tagore: (1861-1941) Indian writer and philosopher, who wrote in the Bengali language; the first Indian to be awarded the Nobel Prize for Literature

Alfred Lord Tennyson: (1809-1892) Poet laureate during Queen Victoria's reign

Mother Teresa: (1910-1997) Albanian Loreto nun of volunteer poverty who offered compassion to the unloved and destitute; started the Sisters of Charity in Calcutta, India

James Thurber: (1894-1961) American cartoonist, author, journalist, playwright and popular humorist

J.R.R. Tolkien: (1892-1973) John Ronald Revel Tolkien was a British writer, poet, philologist, and teacher of medieval literature and language at Oxford University; *The Hobbit; The Lord of the Rings Trilogy*

Eckhart Tolle: (1948--) German born resident of Canada; known for *The Power of Now* and *A New Earth*

Leo Tolstoy: (1828-1910) Influential Russian author, philosopher, and social critic whose great epics include *War and Peace*, his philosophy of non-violence and a return to rural simplicity inspired Gandhi

Brian Tracy: (1944--) Motivational speaker and writer; CEO of Brian Tracy International, which trains and develops individuals and organizations

Harry S. Truman: (1884-1972) The 33rd President of the United States after President Franklin D. Roosevelt died

Mark Twain: (1835-1910) Pen name for Samuel Langhorne Clemens; U.S. author and humorist; *The Adventures of Tom Sawyer and the Adventures of Huckleberry Finn*

V

Leonardo da Vinci: (1452-1519) Italian painter, engineer, musician, and scientist who is considered one of the greatest minds in human history; he painted the most iconic picture in history, "The Mona Lisa"

Virgil: (70 B.C.-19 B.C.) Publius Vergilius Maro was an ancient Roman poet of the Augustan period; *The Aneid*

Voltaire: (1694-1778) Francois-Marie Arovet was a French Enlightenment freemason writer, historian, and philosopher; *Candide*

W

Margaret Walker (1915-1998) African American 20th century author and poet

Izaak Walton: (1594-1683) British author who published biographies of leading figures in *The Compleat Angler*

William Arthur Ward: (1921-1994) Author of *Fountains of Faith*

Rick Warren: (1954--) Minister, author, and philanthropist; *The Purpose Driven Life*

Booker T. Washington: (1856-1915) African American educator who founded the Tuskegee Institute

George Washington: (1732-1799) First President of the United States and a leader of Colonial opposition to British policies in America

Martha Washington: (1731-1802) The very first Lady of the United States

Daniel Webster: (1782-1852) U.S. senator, orator, lawyer, and key Whig leader who gained fame for his eloquent speeches delivered in courtrooms and in Congress

Simone Weil: (1909-1943) French philosopher and religious author

John Wesley: (1703-1791) English theologian, evangelist, and founder of the Methodist church

Edith Wharton: (1862-1937) Pulitzer-Prize winning American novelist, short story writer, and designer; *The Age of Innocence*

William Wilberforce: (1759-1833) Fought tirelessly to end the slave trade

Oscar Wilde: (1854-1900) Irish author, playwright, and poet; *The Picture of Dorian Gray*

Laura Ingalls Wilder: (1867-1957) American writer; *Little House on the Prairie*

Woodrow Wilson: (1856-1924) Thomas Woodrow Wilson was the 28th President of the United States who led the nation through World War I

Walter Winchell: (1897-1972) American newspaper and radio gossip commentator

Oprah Winfrey: (1954--) American media proprietor, talk show host, actress, producer, and philanthropist; *The Oprah Winfrey Show*

Frank Lloyd Wright: (1867-1959) American architect; interior designer, writer and educator

Y

William Butler Yeats: (1865-1939) Irish poet and senator; force behind the Irish Literary Revival; won the 1923 Nobel Prize in Literature

Malala Yousafzai: (1997--) Pakistani schoolgirl who defied threats of the Taliban to campaign for the right to education; she survived being shot by the Taliban and has become a global advocate for women's rights

Z

Zig Ziglar: (1926-2012) American author, salesman, and motivational speaker; *See You at the Top*

World Proverbs

*"The wisdom of nations
lies in their proverbs,
which are brief and pithy."*

William Penn

Afghanistan: Don't show me the palm tree; show me the dates.

A bad wound heals, but a bad word doesn't.

Africa: A camel never sees its own hump.

Do not look where you fell, but where you slipped.

Albania: Don't put gold buttons on a torn coat.

Measure thrice, cut once.

Algeria: Do bad and remember; do good and forget.

A sensible enemy is better than a narrow-minded friend.

American Samoa: The coconut tree doesn't sway on its own, but is swayed by the wind.

May your mind be like cool water.

Andorra: Cast no dirt into the well that gives you water.

The best word is the unspoken word.

Angola: It is the voyage, not the ship that matters.

The one who throws the stone forgets; the one who is hit remembers.

Anguilla: A crab never forget he hole.

All cassava get same skin, but all nah taste same way.

Antigua and Barbuda: Clothes cover character.

Black hens can lay white eggs.

Argentina: If you have a tail of straw, then keep away from the fire.

It takes two to tango.

Armenia: You are as many a person as languages you
know.

The only sword that never rests is the tongue of a
woman.

Aruba: As the old ones sing, so do the young ones chirp.

Never believe someone who carries fire in one hand
and water in the other.

Australia: He that hurts another hurts himself.

The family that prays together stays together.

Austria: What I do not know will not keep me warm.

The earth does not shake when the flea coughs.

Bahamas, The: A strawberry will not sweeten dry bread.

To engage in conflict, one does not bring a knife
that cuts but a needle that sews.

Bahrain: All you have is your nose, even if it's a bent one.

What's in the pan the spoon will dig out.

Bangladesh: To endure is obligatory, but to like it is not.

Half-truth is more dangerous than falsehood.

Barbados: Crave all, get none at all.

Make sure better than cock sure.

Belarus: Fear the law, not the judge.

Everything tastes bitter to him with gall in his mouth.

Belgium: The horse must graze where it is tethered.

It is no use waiting for your ship to come in unless you have sent one out.

Belize: Don't hang your hat higher than you can reach.

Every fat bird has his day.

Benin: Words are like spears; once they leave your lips they can never come back.

When you give you get ten times over.

Bermuda: What you do in the dark will come into the light.

A cockroach has no business in a fowl's dance.

Bhutan: Every bird flies with its own wings.

It is better to walk around a bush than fight with a dog.

Bolivia: If you marry wise judgment, peace will become your brother-in-law.

An altercation is like buttermilk; the more you stir it, the sourer it gets.

Bosnia and Herzegovina: The eyes of all cheats are full of tears.

A pear tree cannot bear an apple.

Botswana: If you live in a mud hut, beware of the rain.

A fool and water will go the way they are diverted.

Brazil: A wise man learns at the fool's expense.

Others will measure you with the same rod you use to measure them.

Brunei: Where there is grass, there are grasshoppers.

When hearts fall out of favor, honey tastes like vinegar.

Bulgaria: Nature, time, and patience are the three great physicians.

A tree falls the way it leans.

Burkina Faso: When carrying an elephant's flesh on one's back, one should not look for crickets underground.

An axe doesn't cut down a tree by itself.

Burma: A hero only appears once the tiger is dead.

Seek wisdom like a beggar.

Burundi: Who made the drum knows best what is inside.

You cannot hide the smoke of the hut you set on fire.

Cabo Verde: Where there is love there is no darkness.

Trees bend when they are young.

Cambodia: You don't have to cut a tree down to get at its fruit.

Don't take the straight path or the winding path. Take the path your ancestors have taken.

Cameroon: A chattering bird builds no nest.

A cherry year, a merry year; a plum year, a dumb year.

Canada: Do not yell "dinner" until your knife is in the loaf.

Walk a mile in my moccasins to learn where they pinch.

Cape Verde: A big head is a big load.

Rats don't dance in the cat's doorway.

Central African Republic: He who thinks he is leading and has no one following him is only taking a walk.

In the moment of crises, the wise build bridges and the foolish build dams.

Chad: Every cock is a town crier in his own dung heap.

Only when a tree is big and strong can you tether a cow to it.

Chile: If you want the dog, accept the fleas.

The dog that doesn't walk doesn't find a bone.

China: A wise man adapts himself to circumstances, as water shapes itself to the vessel that holds it.

Don't stand by the water and long for fish; go home and weave a net.

Colombia: He who must die, must die in the dark, even though he sells candles.

There is no better friend than a burden.

Comoros: A chicken with beautiful plumage does not sit in the corner.

A thread follows the path of the needle.

Congo, Republic of: Don't buy a boat that is under water.

A single bracelet does not jingle.

Cook Islands: It is the octopus who says sitting is working.
The kumara [sweet potato] does not say how sweet it is.

Costa Rica: He that was born as a flute will not become a clarinet.

Envy shoots at others and wounds herself.

Côte d'ivoire: In the village you don't know, the chickens have teeth.

Until the snake is dead, do not drop the stick.

Croatia: Habit is a good servant but a poor master.

An empty barrel sings in the wind.

Cuba: Cheese, wine and a friend must be old to be good.

Listen to what they say of the others and you will know what they say about you.

Cyprus: Friday's mirth is Saturday's grief.

The good captain shows himself in a storm.

Czech Republic: The big thieves hang the little ones.

Do not protect yourself with a fence, but rather by your friends.

Democratic Republic of the Congo: Marriage is a school.

A funeral offers the opportunity for reconciliation.

Denmark: He who builds according to every man's advice will have a crooked house.

He is most cheated who cheats himself.

Djibouti: What an adult sees from the ground, a boy cannot see even if he climbs a silk-cotton tree.

Rather than get up and do a bad dance, stay put.

Dominican Republic: Until the nail is hit, it doesn't believe in the hammer.

A good surgeon must have a hawk's eye, a lion's heart, and a woman's hand.

Ecuador: In youth we learn; in old age we understand.

He who hears no advice will not reach old age.

Equatorial Guinea: Your beauty will take you there, but
your character will bring you back.

A butterfly that flies among thorns will tear its
wings.

Egypt: The barking of a dog does not disturb the man on a
camel.
There grows no wheat where there is no grain.

El Salvador: A tree born crooked will never straighten its
trunk.

It is better to be the head of a mouse than a lion's
tail.

Eritrea: If an enemy learns your dance, he/she dances it
the crooked way.

Tomorrow is pregnant and no one knows what she
will give birth to.

Estonia: The poor beggar is the one who begs without a bag.

Who does not obey the parents' word will be taught
by the world.

Ethiopia: Advise and counsel him; if he does not listen, let adversity teach him.

Only a fool looks for dung where the cattle doesn't graze.

Falkland Islands: Empty vessels make the most sound.

Don't bite the hand that feeds you.

Faroe Islands: None reaches further than his arms reach.

He who waits gets a tailwind, and he who rows, a harbor.

Fiji Islands: Life is like this: sometimes sun, sometimes rain.

Idleness is to be dead at the limbs but alive within.

Finland: One shouldn't make a bull out of a fly.

An accident won't arrive with a bell on its neck.

France: Write injuries in sand, kindnesses in marble.

A man is known by the company he keeps.

French Polynesia: The egg belongs to the hen that cackles.

Don't blow the horn until the bread is baked.

Gabon: A fool looks for dung where the cow never browsed.

To one who does not know, a small garden is a forest.

Gambia, The: The plant protected by God is never hurt by the wind.

If a donkey kicks you, and you kick back, you are both donkeys.

Georgia: If you give a man nuts, then give him something to crack them with.

The buzzing of the flies does not turn them into bees.

Germany: Where there are no swamps there are no frogs.

The wise man has long ears and a short tongue.

Ghana: If things are getting easier, maybe you're headed downhill.

Only when you have crossed the river can you say the crocodile has a lump on his snout.

Gibraltar: He who eats with the devil must have a long spoon.

Make hay while the sun shines.

Great Britain: A big tree attracts the woodsman's axe.

Loose lips sink ships.

Greece: Milk the cow, but do not pull off the udder.

Men who have lost heart never yet won a trophy.

Greenland: When you have gone so far that you can't manage one more step, then you've gone just half the distance that you're capable of.

A kajak hunter who has a beautiful wife comes early home from hunting.

Grenada: A new broom sweeps clean, but an old broom knows the corners.

An empty sack can't stand up; a full sack cannot bend.

Guadeloupe: A good funeral does not lead to paradise.

The tree does not rot on the day it fell in the water.

Guam: Don't take the catch from another's trap.

The more liberty, the more license.

Guatemala: Whoever does not teach his son a useful art teaches stealing.

When you point your finger, remember that three fingers point back at you.

Guinea, Republic of: The toad likes water but not when it is boiling.

The man on his feet carries off the share of the man sitting down.

Guyana: Never shop for black cloth at nighttime.

Don't wait until you want to urinate to build a toilet.

Haiti: Do not insult the mother alligator until after you have crossed the river.

A borrowed drum never makes good dancing.

Hawaii: All knowledge is not taught in one school.

Do not stir up water that is still.

Holland: A handful of patience is worth more than a bushel of brains.

Don't throw away your old shoes until you have got new ones.

Honduras: When the blind leads the way, woe to those who
    follow.

The hare jumps when you least expect it.

Hong Kong: Do not fear going forward slowly; fear only
    to stand still.

A rat who gnaws at a cat's tail invites destruction.

Hungary: A prudent man does not make the goat his
    gardener.

Bargain like a gypsy, but pay like a gentleman.

Iceland: He who lives without discipline dies without honor.

A man without a book is blind.

India: Call on God, but row away from the rocks.

The poor looks for food and the rich man for
appetite.

Indonesia: No matter how good a squirrel can jump, it
    will fall eventually.

Different fields, different grasshoppers; different
seas, different fish.

Iran: If you live in the river you should make friends with crocodiles.

A timely tear is better than a misplaced smile.

Iraq: One who is drowning will even grab onto a snake.

Someone who does not know how to dance will say the ground is sloping.

Ireland: You've got to do your own growing, no matter how tall your grandfather was.

It's no use carrying an umbrella if your shoes are leaking.

Israel: A pessimist, confronted with two bad choices, chooses both.

You can't force anyone to love you or to lend you money.

Italy: Once the game is over, the king and the pawn go back in the same box.

To every bird, his own nest is beautiful.

Jamaica: When you go to a donkey's house, don't talk about ears.

Today can't catch tomorrow.

Japan: You can't see the whole sky through a bamboo tube.

> When the character of a man is not clear to you, look at his friends.

Jordan: A promise is a cloud; fulfillment is rain.

> In the desert of life the wise person travels by caravan while the fool prefers to travel alone.

Kazakhstan: Iron is tested in fire, and the person in distress.

> There is no place like your Motherland.

Kenya: A friend is someone who knows the song in your heart and can sing it back to you when you have forgotten the words.

> All monkeys cannot hang on the same branch.

Kirbati: You are like a school of sardines—so many and good for only one bite.

> A man should not go back on his word.

Korea, Democratic People's Republic (North Korea): Even if you encounter a stone bridge, tap it first before crossing.

> Do not draw your sword to kill a fly.

Korea, Republic of (South Korea): If you kick a stone in anger, you'll hurt your own foot.

Aim high in your career, but stay humble in your heart.

Kosovo: If you are quick to believe, you'll be quickly deceived.

Where people are promising you much, bring a small bag.

Kuwait: I complained because I had no shoes until I met a man who had no feet.

A known mistake is better than an unknown truth.

Kyrgyzstan: The earth is a small place for fugitives.

If your right hand is angry, hold it back with your left.

Latvia: A smiling face is half the meal.

In dense woods the trees grow straight.

Lebanon: Lower your voice and strengthen your argument.

A donkey is a donkey though it may carry the sultan's treasure.

Laos: One piece of wood will not make a fire.

The voice of a poor man does not carry very far.

Lesotho: Houses built together burn together.

> Do not laugh at the snake because it walks on its belly.

Liberia: The hen who never stays in the nest never hatches the chick.

> A bird and a fish can get married, but where will they build their nest?

Libya: Maliciously acquired gold never lasts long.

> All that is round is not a cake.

Liechtenstein: Charity sees the need not the cause.

> Speaking comes by nature, silence by understanding.

Lithuania: Offer the lazy an egg, and they'll want you to peel it for them.

> Gold glitters even in the mud.

Luxembourg: Where there is no temptation there is no glory.

> Honey is sweet, but the bees sting.

Macedonia, Republic of: Where force rules, justice does not exist.

> The brain is not in the pocket, but in the head.

Madagascar: Words are like eggs. When they are hatched, they have wings.

A chicken that hatches a crocodile's egg is looking for trouble.

Malawi: When you are on the back of an elephant, don't pretend there is no dew on the grass.

Do not be like the mosquito that bites the owner of the house.

Malaysia: Don't think there are no crocodiles just because the water is calm.

Bleat when you are in the goat pen and moo when you are in the buffalo pen.

Maldives: The robber's trunk is tightly shut.

The water pot that is full will not shake.

Mali: A deaf man may not have heard the hunger, but he surely will see the rain.

A bee forced into a beehive will not make any honey.

Malta: Where the heart loves, there the legs walk.

Chasten thy son while there is hope.

Marshall Islands: Drops together make the ocean, and grains of sand together make an island.

Don't paddle over groupers, for there are groupers below.

Martinique: The kicking of the mare does not hurt the horse.

Jealousy is the sister of witchcraft.

Mauritania: The sheep that wants to grow a long horn must have a strong skull.

If you watch your pot, your food will not burn.

Mauritius: What you lose in the fire, you will find in the ashes.

A hen cannot lay eggs and hatch them in the same day.

Mexico: Envious persons never compliment; they only swallow.

A good resolution is like an old horse, which is often saddled but rarely ridden.

Micronesia: One cannot eat the meat of every bird.

The moon is not shamed by the barking of dogs.

Moldova, Republic of: It's the tone that makes the song.

One doesn't make a donkey drink if it isn't thirsty.

Monaco: Nothing is impossible with a willing heart.

True love never grows old.

Mongolia: There are men who walk through the woods and see no trees.

It is easier to catch an escaped horse than to take back an escaped word.

Montenegro: Winter finds out what summer lays up.

He who wakes up early catches two fortunes.

Morocco: Do not correct with a strike that which can be taught with a kiss.

The heart of a fool is in his mouth; the mouth of a wise man is in his heart.

Mozambique: There are no shortcuts to the top of the palm tree.

There is no elephant that complains about the weight of its trunk.

Myanmar: Collect the water while it rains.

> You can stop speaking to someone, but you cannot stop being related.

Namibia: Do not leave your host's house throwing mud in his well.

> A hunter who has only one arrow does not shoot with careless aim.

Nepal: The one who is guilty has the higher voice.

> Thunderclouds do not always give rain.

Netherlands: Little pots soon run over.

> A handful of patience is worth more than a bushel of brains.

New Zealand: The block of wood should not dictate to the carrier.

> Persist as resolutely as you persist in eating.

Nicaragua: It takes two to make a quarrel but only one to end it.

> Eyes that see do not grow old.

Niger: Abundance will make cotton pull a stone.

> The cry of the hyena and the loss of the goat are one.

Nigeria: However far the stream flows it never forgets its source.

Water can cover the footprint on the ground but it does not cover the words of the mouth.

Niue: Don't count the chickens yet in case the eggs are rotten.
Put clothes on your words.

Northern Mariano Islands: Try it lest you be fooled.

The more you talk the more you lie.

Norway: Luck is loaned, not owned.

Rather a bit correctly than much incorrectly.

Oman: A man without a plan is like a gun without a bullet.

Choose your neighbor before you choose your house.

Pakistan: Good manners are your beauty.

A friend appears in hard times, not at big dinners.

Palau: A great leader is like the rain that calms the ocean.

You are like a school of sardines, so many and good for only one bite.

Palestinian Territories: Your close neighbor is better than your faraway brother.

The eye cannot rise above the eyebrow.

Panama: Among the weak, the strongest is the one who doesn't forget his weakness.

Half an orange tastes just as sweet as a whole one.

Papua New Guinea: The fishing net is knotted at night, but untangled in the morning.

Gather the breadfruit from the farthest branch first.

Paraguay: Rare is the person who can weigh faults of another without putting his thumb on the scales.

A hatchet in the mouth is more harmful than a hatchet in the hand.

Peru: Only he who carries it knows how much the cross weighs.

When the road is long, even slippers feel tight.

Philippines: The rattan basket criticizes the palm leaf basket; still both are full of holes.

Tell me who your friends are and I'll tell you who you are.

Pitcairn Island: The shark will not give up his food.

> The dog that doesn't walk doesn't find a bone.

Poland: A fault confessed is half redressed.

> There are a thousand paths to every wrong.

Portugal: Every peddler praises his own needles.

> It's when it's small that the cucumber gets warped.

Puerto Rico: Break the leg of a bad habit.

> Nobody knows what's in the pot but the one who's stirring it.

Qatar: Who went without an invitation will sleep without a blanket.

> Those who cannot reach the grape will say it is sour.

Réunion Island: It is in the old bowls that makes good soup.

> I love you like a pig loves his mud.

Romania: Do not put your spoon into the pot, which does not boil for you.

> A cock is bold on his own dunghill.

Russian Federation: A spoken word is not a sparrow. Once it flies out, you can't catch it.

Pray to God, but keep rowing to the shore.

Rwanda: In a court of fowls, the cockroach never wins a case.

When your beard appears, childhood disappears.

Saint Kitts and Nevis: One hand can't clap.

Today can't catch tomorrow.

Saint Lucia: The stroke of a cutlass in water leaves no mark.

A sunken ship won't prevent another's sailing.

Saint Vincent and the Grenadines: There is a great distance between said and done.

Pay the doctor; praise the Lord.

Samoa: You shake in vain the branch that bears no fruit.

Coral blocks have nothing to do with the preparation of masi.

San Marino: Bad company is what brings men to the gallows.

The dogs bark but the caravan passes by.

Sao Tome and Principe: A fool's tongue is long enough to cut his own throat.

The frog does not drink up the pond in which he lives.

Saudi Arabia: A book is a garden carried in the pocket.

If you oppress who is below you, you won't be safe from the punishment of who is above you.

Scotland: Children speak in the field what they hear in the house.

Never let your feet run faster than your shoes.

Senegal: If a centipede loses a leg, it does not prevent him from walking.

If the eyes do not admire, the heart will not desire.

Serbia: A greedy father has thieves for children.

It is better to be threatened by the sword of a Turk than by the pen of a German.

Seychelles: Crooked wood is straightened with fire.

It's not worth adding water to the sea.

Sierra Leone: The big fish is caught with big bait.

A fish has nothing to do with a raincoat.

Singapore: If you plant grass, you won't get rice.

    Not all stones are blessed to become diamonds.

Slovakia (Slovah Republic): Others read your face, God your heart.

    The one who first shuts up in an argument is from a good family.

Slovenia: Never whisper to the deaf or wink at the blind.

    A doorstep is the highest of all mountains.

Solomon Islands: If they heard there was a wedding in the sky, women would try to put up a ladder.

    An iron sharpens iron as a pal sharpens a buddy.

Somalia: He who does not shame you does not cut you.

    In the ocean, one does not need to sow water.

South Africa: The fool who owns an ox is seldom recognized as a fool.

    Behold the iguana puffing itself out to make itself a man!

South Sudan: A fool will not even find water at the Nile.

    It is a fool who rejoices when the neighbor is in trouble.

Spain: Books are hindrances to persisting stupidity.

He who goes with wolves learns to howl.

Sri Lanka: For he who has the time even the jungle is paradise.

He who has studied himself is his own master.

Sudan: God gives nothing to those who keep their arms crossed.

Eggs and iron must not be in the same bag.

Suriname: The child that does not cry does not get milk from its mother.

When the wind blows, you see the fowl's back.

Svalbard: Good fortune is loaned, now owned.

The lame runs if he has to.

Swaziland: A person who says it cannot be done should not interrupt the man doing it.

When a gorilla is in power, the monkeys are happy.

Sweden: Don't throw away the old bucket until you know whether the new one holds water.

One should go invited to a friend in good fortune and uninvited in misfortune.

Switzerland: Speech is silver; silence is golden.

> Sometimes you have to be silent in order to be heard.

Syria (Syrian Arab Republic): You should fear the one who does not fear God.

> The person who deals in camels should make the doors high.

Taiwan: It takes sweat to work on things, but it only takes saliva to criticize things.

> As long as you have the forest, you don't have to worry about firewood.

Tajikstan: When the father's work is done, the result is a well-trained son.

> The sun cannot be covered by a skirt.

Tanzania: The roaring lion kills no game.

> Do not mend your neighbor's fence before looking to your own.

Thailand: At high tide fish eat ants; at low tide ants eat fish.

> Catch a fish with two hands.

Tibet: Rebellious thoughts are like an abandoned house overtaken by robbers.

> Don't trust a hungry man to watch your rice.

Togo: Breed up a serpent and he will strike when you are in deep slumber.

You can't scare a monkey with a dead baboon.

Tonga: He who provokes a war must be sure that he knows how to fight.

The hyena does not forget where it has hidden its kill.

Tovalu: The gratitude of a donkey is a kick.

Don't set sail using somebody else's star.

Trinidad and Tobago: What the eyes don't see the heart don't grieve.

What ears hear tongue shouldn't know.

Tunisia: Unwatched wealth teaches stealth.
Never dive before you measure.

Turkey: Having two ears and one tongue, we should listen twice as much as we speak.

For the birds that cannot soar, God has provided low branches.

Turkmenistan: Walk barefoot and the thorns will hurt you.

The person who spends time with the lame learns how to limp.

Turks and Caicos Islands: Goat business is not the business of sheep.

If you saw what the river carried, you would never drink the water.

Uganda: The hunter in pursuit of an elephant does not stop to throw stones at birds.

Water that has been begged for does not quench the thirst.

Ukraine: No matter how hard you try the bull will never give milk.

The mother remembers her youth and so does not trust her daughter.

United Arab Emirates: He who wants to sell his honor will always find a buyer.

Trust God, but always tie up your camel.

United Kingdom: Birds of a feather flock together.

One man's meat is another man's poison.

United States of America: After all is said and done, more is said than done.

In trying times, don't quit trying.

Uruguay: Gifts break rocks and melt hearts.

> Better to lose a minute of your life than your life in a minute.

Uzbekistan: Who speaks a little knows a lot, and when he speaks, it's with great thought.

> Good breeding and good grace are not sold in the marketplace.

Vanuatu: A heart deep in love has no patience.

> If you love a pumpkin, also love its flower.

Vatican City: (Holy See): No one is truly poor except the one who lacks the truth.

> Unhappy is the soul enslaved by the love of anything that is mortal.

Venezuela, Bolivarian Republic of: A good friend will fit you like a ring to a finger.

> Those who get up early are helped by God.

Virgin Islands (British): Time is longer than a rope.

> Jack of all trades is master of none.

Virgin Islands (U.S.): Dirty water can put out fire.

> All fish does bite, but shark does get the blame.

Vietnam: There is one fish in the pond and ten anglers on the bank.

Young bamboo trees are easy to bend.

Wales: Bad news goes about in clogs; good news in stockinged feet.

Anger is the mother of treachery.

Western Sahara: Patience is the key to paradise.

Not all the flowers of a tree produce fruit.

Yemen: A mule driver is not aware of the stink of his animals.

If speech is of silver, silence is golden.

Yugoslavia, Federal Republic of: No one likes to be the first to step on the ice.

When the big bells ring, the little bells are not heard.

Zambia: To get rid of anger, first weed out the bitter roots.

Where God cooks, there is no smoke.

Zimbabwe: If you can walk you can dance; if you can talk you can sing.

God is good, but never dance with a lion.

www.ingramcontent.com/pod-product-compliance
Lightning Source LLC
Chambersburg PA
CBHW030009290326
41934CB00005B/273